I0413333

THE EPIPHANY OF JILLIAN ASHTON

A 16 Year Old Girl's Dilemma
The Acceptance of Truth or Denial of Lies

DENIAL, UNDERSTANDING, RETRIBUTION

AND VINDICATION

Dedicated to my children, grandchildren and all
Of the young people now burdened with the "gift"
Of debt given to them by the administration and the
Congress that provided little leadership, while they
Held power as of January 2009 and hopefully ending

January 2016

ISBN-13:978-1495474620
ISBN-10:1495474623

PROLOGUE

The School The Hamlet

The Endicott Witherspoon Preparatory School, a non-denominational school for intermediate education, and originally a school for boys was founded in 1983 with moneys endowed by Agnes Endicott Witherspoon heir to a vast fortune earned by oil exploration and development. Having died in 1980, Miss Witherspoon never saw the fruits of her generosity. Ten years later, understanding the need for additional money and pressured to become politically correct, the school opened its doors to young girls.

Located in the hamlet of Hurley, in the town of Hurley and abutting the town of Woodstock, the school sits high above a valley, in a wilderness that begins where its access Gallis Hill Road ends. With New York City barely 100 miles to the south and ample available bus and train transportation, students from more affluent families have been provided housing on the vast campus, while the majority of students reside within a 20 mile radius.

The hamlet of Hurley, considered as such, because it is a community within the unincorporated town of Hurley, just west of Kingston, the Revolutionary capitol of New York State, is dependent upon its namesake for both municipal services and government. The area was established in 1669 by Peter Stuyvesant, and after a series of Indian wars, in 1708, was resettled and named after Francis Lovelace, Baron of Hurley, in Ireland.

In the last government census, it was concluded that the hamlet consisted of 1415 households, of which 1049 were families. 95.7% were White, 1.24% were Black, 0.11% were Asian, and 2.13% were Hispanic. Twenty-three percent were noted to be less than 18 years of age. 62% were married and living together. 11.5% of people over age 65 lived alone.

In 2012, it was determined that 2.3% of the population were below the poverty level earning less than $23,050 per year.

The largest number of students came from Saugerties, Woodstock and its adjacent communities of Shady, and Willow, although there was a group from Palenville and Tannersville that contributed a fifth of the lower classes.

Woodstock and its environs, once a bastion of conservative thought, had become considerably liberal over the past twenty years. Under the implied threat of boycott, many local business people found it expedient to hide their concerns over the impending loss of freedoms and what they perceived as federal government oppression. Because of overt liberal teaching in schools by teachers who espoused the new liberal progressivism, small wars broke out between husbands and wives, brothers and sisters, once close friends, as well as parents and their impressionable teenagers.

ONE

The Assignment

Jillian Ashton raced up the stairs taking two steps at a time, as the class bell rang for the third and last time. Having Physical Education first period on Thursday, had become an assault on her personal hygiene, so she stopped at her locker for some deodorant to offset what she believed others might find offensive. If the entire Current History class had to deal with what she felt she had to deal with, there would be no issue, or so she believed. Out of breath she entered the classroom, and found that the teacher, Davida Jones had not yet arrived. On her desk, however was a pile of blue books, normally used in end of semester tests for writing essays.

She sat at her desk and placed her backpack on the floor, as her friend Faith Morton looked up from her IPad.

"Teach is late again. You just made it in time." The pretty blonde said, as a tall woman entered the classroom, carrying more blue books. The students, who had started to stir, suddenly quieted as she glared at them.

She piled the books on top of the ones already on her desk, and went right to the blackboard, writing the word ASSIGNMENT. Davida Jones turned back toward the class and registered a smile of sorts. Picking up fresh chalk, she wrote WHY PRESIDENT OBAMA SHOULD BE CONSIDERED ONE OF THE GREAT PRESIDENTS AND LEADERS OF THE UNITED STATES. Sitting down behind her desk she pointed at the blue books.

With a strong New Yaawk intonation, she said. "Take as many of these books you require. There is no limit on words. Oh, and please with exquisite English." She smiled.

5

5

"Be advised that you will have twenty-one days to complete the essay, and it will represent the bulk of your grade, so do a good job and write appropriately. You will be thinking seriously about colleges soon. Single spaced on your computer and printed out will be okay, but you must turn in the originals in your own handwriting in the blue books. Any questions?"

A friend of Jillian's, from Saugerties, Sasha Finkel, raised her eyebrows, but did not dare ask the question she had on her mind. 'What if I think he is just a fraud? How does that reconcile with the assignment.' Sasha did not wish to create a wave of dissent. After all, she had long ago decided to follow in her father's footsteps, attend a university with a medical school and become a Pediatrician. She knew of ten of her classmates, who felt as she did politically, who also knew it less than expedient to challenge Ms. Jones. Jillian was another problem for Sasha, since she liked her despite her blind advocacy of the Obama administration, and just accepted the fact that it was a result of living in Woodstock. She could not comprehend why Jillian's father, a hospital attorney, and her mother, a registered nurse, would be accepting of such "tyranny" as the Affordable Health Care law, aka obamacare. Jillian had once gone as far as suggesting that Obama's likeness should be placed alongside Washington, Jefferson, Roosevelt and Lincoln on Mt. Rushmore.

After forty-five minutes of what Sasha believed to be a rearrangement of history, they were saved by the bell and hurried as a group to their Humanities class one floor below.

Later in the cafeteria, eight junior girls and Nancy Dick's, boyfriend Tony Grieg, a senior, sat around a table eating lunch. Sasha and Jillian picked at what was called a vegetable medley, while the other seven ate illegal sandwiches they had secreted in their backpacks.

"Medley!" Tony snorted. "Sure looks to me like total discord. Why are you still eating rabbit food? And what happened to the pizza and burgers our folks paid for?"

Mandy Van Wagoner took a bite of tuna sandwich and leaned forward. "You know," she whispered, "I spend lots a time in the office since I'm a hall monitor. Well, I know for a fact that old Endy Withers is hoping for a major grant of money from the Federal Government. So I guess if 'you know who' thinks we are eating how she wants us to, she might talk hubby into opening up the purse."

Jillian frowned and tossed the last of her carrots and apple into a nearby trashcan. "You know nothing of the kind and that is deceitful. If you want to remain friends, all of you, don't say such hurtful things about the president."

Sasha smiled. "Look I have a great idea about how to do the essays. Since there is so much to go through and we have barely three weeks, I suggest we divide up the issues and deal with them collectively."

"Great idea," Nancy remarked. "I don't plan to spend all of my waking days on this, and Tony and I have plans for a weekend in the city to see a few shows."

"The whole weekend?" Victoria Morales laughed. "Your folks aware of this?

"Grow up!" Nancy retorted. "As it is they are coming with us."

"Okay, about doing the essay as I suggested. There are thirty more juniors with the same assignment. We could all help each other out." Sasha said.

Jillian looked skeptical. "I don't know that this legal and if we are found out…"

"Sasha smirked. "We all write our own essays. We are just using different resources to gather information. Hey. It is no different than You Google me and I Google you."

Tony laughed. "Sound's absolutely sexual. Count me in."

"You don't have to write one, so cut it out," Sasha said.

"Well," Tony answered. "I am in Senior Honors political science. I can really help. Uh! Better change the subject."

At that moment Ms. Jones sat her tray on a table next to theirs. "So what are you plotting?" She inquired.

Later, after their last class, the nine met in the parking lot. Sasha was to be picked up by her older brother. Tony would drive Nancy home, and the others would wait for the bus that would take them back to Woodstock.

"This is the plan," Sasha said. I will call you tonight. Since all of you live in Woodstock, I am willing to come to meet with all of you to work out the specifics."

Jillian smiled wryly at her eight friends, but shook her head. I haven't agreed to anything. But, I will speak to my Dad about it."

"Look Jillian," Sasha said as her brother drove up in a black Lexus, "this is only as political as each of us plans to make it. After all, information is just information and the truth is just the truth." She got into the car and her brother moved out of the parking lot as a yellow bus came to a halt nearby.

The bus dropped Jillian off near Ricks Road. As she walked the three hundred feet to her home, her mother drove up in her new Subaru Forrester. "Need a ride young lady."

She helped Jennie Ashton unload groceries from the back of the car, and clapped her hands. "Wonderful, I am so pizza starved. Is it for tonight?"

The four Australian sheepdogs greeted them, as they turned the key in the front door, as if it had been years since they had last seen them. "All right. Let's calm down now." Jennie said. "Why don't you fill their dishes and get that over with. I am waiting for a call from your father. There was an urgent matter he had to deal with at the hospital."

Shane, Shelby, Kodi and Ranger tried to beat Jillian down the short flight of stairs that led to the kitchen and their dinner, which was actually the same as breakfast, but they acted as if they did not know. It took three minutes to fill four dishes and a minute and a half for them to empty them.

Jennie put away the groceries and went back into the living room where she opened a bottle of Merlot, poured herself a glass and sat down in a soft chair. She grabbed the remote, turned on the TV and dialed in Fox News.

Jillian had changed into a long sleeve shirt and sweats. She was barefoot. When she saw what Jennie was watching, she raised both hands to cover her ears. "Do we have to watch that?" She asked.

"Darling, you have your own television in your room and are free, well almost free to watch what you want. It's been a long day, and I need to relax."

"You call watching them beating up on the president relaxing?" Jillian asked.

"No one is misspeaking on Fox, Jillian. I don't recall you ever watching Fox." Her mother said and sipped from her glass.

"Well, I never watched it. But I certainly heard all about how terrible they were from Ms. Jones." Jillian said.

"I see," said Jennie. "So you just choose to believe what other people tell you instead of hearing it with your own ears and making an intelligent decision."

"Oh, you know how it is." Jillian said. "Are we having that pizza?"

"Actually I know more than you think, both your father and I, since we are willing to find out what is really going on in this country. People happy to live their own little narrow world, and ask no questions, deserve all of the terrible things that government might do to them. We refuse to allow ourselves to wallow in their mud. The pizza is in the fridge. It will be dinner twenty minutes after your father comes home. He works very hard for all of us."

"You both do and I love you and appreciate everything you and Daddy have done for Mark and me. Oh, have you heard from my brother?"

Jennie rose and refilled her glass. "Actually, Mark will be home tomorrow to spend the weekend, and he is bringing a girl friend."

"A girl friend. Can't wait." Jillian said. "Mom. That's your second glass. Tough day today?

"And my last for the evening. I was switched to the Brain Trauma unit for two weeks. Those poor people. We are doing the best we can with the resources we have. They reduce staff everyday and more terrible problems are in the offing, but I would think you have little interest in that." Jennie said, as the four Aussies began their attack on the front door announcing the arrival of Stanley Ashton.

He kissed his wife and daughter, hung up his jacket and sat down in his favorite chair, as Jennie brought him a glass of the red wine.

"So I know how my day went. What about the two of you?" Stanley asked.

"Jillian can go first. I'll put the pizza in the oven." Jennie said as she went down to the kitchen.

Jillian took a seat on an ottoman she pushed in front of her father's chair. "Got a new assignment and am a bit perplexed how to approach it." Jillian said.

"Okay," Stanley responded. "So what's the assignment?"

He frowned as she explained what Ms. Jones had assigned the class. "That is what is called a self-fulfilling prophecy." He said.

"I don't understand that, Daddy." She said.

"If I understand it correctly, you are supposed to write an essay in no restricted amount of words as to how great the man is at least in his role as president with that being your only conclusion. Do you have to compare him with other presidents we have had?" He asked. "That could be a good start."

"She didn't say so." Jillian responded. "This is the deal that has me worried. Sasha, you know Sasha from Saugerties, whose family are probably involved with those tea pots."

Stanley interrupted. "I have met both her mother and father, and know that they have conservative views. And it is called the Tea Party and not tea pots."

"Well I hear those people, not necessarily the Finkels, but like them, you know, are racists and hate the president because he is black." Jillian said.

"Jillian. I am so surprised. You have hung around us, and our friends now for almost seventeen years. Where did you ever hear such garbage?" Stanley said angrily.

"I don't mean to get you upset, Daddy. Well I read it in the town paper and I hear it at school as well." She said.

"From whom?" He demanded.

"Well from Ms. Jones, and some of the kids at school." She said.

"I see." He finished his wine and sat back in the chair.

"Ms. Jones is your Current History teacher, yes?" She nodded her head. "And Ms. Jones is um, African-American, yes?" She nodded again, as Jennie started to set the table for dinner.

"You to get washed up if you haven't already. More wine, dear? She asked.

"Thanks, but I have had enough." He said to his wife. "Tell me something, daughter. Might you be afraid that your teacher could possibly give you a bad grade if you did not vomit back the lies she has filled you with?"

Jillian got up. "I don't know that she teaches us lies, but yes, she does hold a lot over us as juniors with college decisions soon to be made. This essay, she said, will be two thirds of the semester grade."

"That makes no sense what so ever. What could she possibly gain if the class wrote an essay favorable to the president?" He was perplexed.

"Daddy, at lunch I heard that the school hopes to get some money from the government, and that's why the food has been so terrible in the cafeteria." Jillian offered.

He rose from the chair and went to the table as Jennie brought the pizza and placed it on a heatproof place setting. "Now, my darling daughter. You are making sense. It is important to question everything you are taught and everything you are told. Nothing should be taken for granted. Least of all what anyone from our government has to say about anything."

Jillian then went on to tell her parents about Sasha's plan, in between bites of pizza that she relished. "But," she offered, "I am a bit scared about doing this, since it might seem that we worked together."

"Well," Stanley said, reaching for another slice that he dusted with hot pepper flakes. "You actually are working together collecting information. Sort of tutoring each other. We did that in college and is not illegal, since you will independently write your essays without assistance, once you are satisfied that you all know everything you need to know."

"I am still worried that if she finds out, Ms. Jones, that is…."Jillian said.

"Well it is time for me to chime in my two cents," Jennie said. "If you ultimately write everything supported by facts to prove your point, almost like a debate, what's the issue?"

"You don't know her." Jillian said.

"I think we know her quite well now. I will make deal with all of you guys. You all read and watch everything past and present about the president, and come up with what ever you decide for your essay, and if there is any problem for anyone, I will back them up pro bono, unless they choose not to use my expertise." Stanley said as he pushed his chair away from the table.

"That means for free. Right." Jillian asked smiling.

"Right you are. That means for free." He said.

"I have no idea where to start." Jillian said in desperation.

"I am prepared to help you by providing the ideas, the issues you must deal with and a list of books and television news programs I expect all of you to read, watch and understand. You are a year away from college and two years away from the right to vote and in some instances fight for this country. You all better have a complete understanding of what is happening to all of us whether you wish to believe, remain in a state of denial, or take a stand to defend our rights as a people." Stanley went over to the bookcase and removed two books that he handed to his daughter.

She looked at both covers. "Jerome R. Corsi, Ph.D. 'The Obamanation' and 'Dreams of My Father', by President Obama. I did not realize he wrote a book."

"Well," he started to say but did not complete the thought. "I also have a book by Glenn Beck called Common Sense, which is excellent. The good news is that your teacher gave you a lot of time to write the essay. The bad news is that you have only twenty-one days to accomplish this, and to do it correctly it will mean about seventeen days of preparation, leaving four for completion."

Jillian gulped. "Oh, my. Nancy, her folks and Tony are spending next weekend in the city. How will they do the work?"

"That will be their problem. You, Sasha and the rest do want to get into the best universities. Right?" Stanley said. "Now are you willing to commit? "

"Yes, Daddy." Jillian said as Her mother squeezed her hand.

"Okay, tonight I make a list of issues you will have to concern yourself with, and in all probability you have never heard of most of them." Stanley took two yellow legal pads from his briefcase, giving Jillian one of them. I will make a list of television news programs you should watch. Yes, the dreaded Fox will be on the list as well as MSNBC, CNN and some programs that promote only comedy and really not news."

"There will be no time for reality shows, those that promote pure Hollywood gossip, and texting will be reduced to a bare minimum. Now you have two resource books for a start. Take copious notes, and keep an open mind, which means you may have to forget some of that stuff your teachers have filled your head with." Stanley looked at his daughter who clutched the two books to her chest. "Agreed?"

"Absolutely," Jillian responded.

"Great." He looked at his watch. "It is only 7 p.m. Go ahead and call your friends, but for now, you don't have to share my little legal deal with them."

It was around 11:40, when Sasha Finkel's iPhone beeped indicating that it had received a text message. Half watching a the beginning of a Jay Leno monologue, she saw it was from Jillian asking her to call her if she was still awake. Jillian answered immediately and told her of the conversation with her father, omitting what he asked her not to share. . Then she explained that she had started to read a book by Jerome Corsi and had some questions. Sasha advised her that she had read the book a while back and found it disturbing as well, but for other reasons.

"All this stuff he says cannot be true." Jillian said.

"Well why don't we look at it this way. Why not?" Sasha responded with a yawn.

"And something else that freaks me out." Jillian added. "I agreed to watch some Fox stuff, and saw parts of Megyn Kelly this evening, since I had finished my math homework in study period. She's really cool. However, she was furious about some issue with obamacare, which I know little about other than it will do a lot providing health insurance for millions without it, save so many lives and cost a lot less."

"Yeah. Right. I saw it as well. There are so many problems with the law, the least being that the website is a disaster, but let's concentrate on that for the moment. What she was angry about was the fact that Obama is prancing about with praise for the fixes in the site, while there is a complete disconnect between the enrollee, his or her personal tax information, and the insurance company that has to insure them, and pay their healthcare bills." Sasha said now fully awake.

"Hold on. You are going too fast for me." Jillian whispered. "It's late. We have school tomorrow, and my brother is coming for the weekend, and with a girl. He was able to switch with another one of the residents."

"Right. Mark is a resident in radiology. I would like to speak to him about the future of medicine as he sees it. If you want an earful about the failure of obamacare, now and what lies ahead, ask him his opinion. A girl, huh? Goodnight Jillian."

Although she did not quite understand all of what had caused Megyn Kelly's anger, she knew that the president had explained why the Healthcare Law would be good for all Americans; however, she did not understand the concept of giving a blank check to insurance companies, because the web site was not quite up to snuff. 'But he has already done such good things', she thought. 'Why not just give it a chance? Such real progress like obamacare, would be a good place to begin, to show that he truly has been a great president.'

TWO

Enlightenment: A Beginning

Before she began the lesson, Ms. Jones took a few minutes to say that she hoped that the class had already started to think about their assignment, and if not, reminded them that there were now only twenty days left in which to do so. Then she added as if it were merely an afterthought.

"I caution all of you to be wary of nay sayers and groups of people whose intent to discredit him, solely because he is an African-American. There is so much information available that one need not watch certain conservative cable stations, listen to obstructive troublemakers on radio or look to the Internet for so-called truths without making sure your facts are correct. In the latter case there is always Snopes." She went to the blackboard and wrote the name in rather large capital letters. "I cannot emphasize how important this assignment might be to all of you." She grinned. "Oh! I neglected to mention that making an outline of issues you plan to discuss, is necessary and has to be on my desk next Monday morning."

The group met in the cafeteria over the noon hour.

"I don't get the point of us staying here for this lunch when we have early dismissal because they all have a curriculum meeting." Tony remarked.

"It's all bull shit, and I am still pissed off that she said what she said. The threat is no longer implied." Sasha said as she pushed her tray away. "I'll eat some real food when I get home."

"As to their meeting, they are probably deciding on what new propaganda to fill our heads with." Jane Logan spoke for the first time. "And why the outline? It is like she is spying on us."

"Look", Nancy said. "My Dad is a democrat as are many of our families. He works for the governor in Albany and has hopes of rising up in the party. I don't know if I can go along with all of this. I won't be a traitor." She started to get up.

"Sit back down, Nancy. We need all of us to write what we really believe." Sasha said. "My dad was a registered democrat for years, mainly because his folks were and their folks way back to when Franklin Roosevelt was president. It was almost as if it was their birthright. Most of my relatives are now registered Republicans who reserve the right to exercise independent thought. We all are part of the future of this country, and we had better have a good idea of what is really going on since it will soon be our turn to vote."

Jillian had sat quietly except for the munching noise her teeth made on the carrot she held in her hand. "We, I, have to keep an open mind, so I am willing to let everything into mine, and plan to sort it all out in the next two weeks. I am of the mind to give Obama the benefit of the doubt. I cannot accept the fact that our teachers and the media would purposefully lie to us."

"Please do not forget the president." Sasha said.

Jillian's face reddened. "The deal is for us to make our own decisions based upon what we learn. Some of you have already done so, but all of must think and write independently. A lot could ride on what we do and write."

The others nodded their heads in agreement.

"When is your brother Mark coming?" Sasha asked. "And is he serious with this girl?"

Jillian's face brightened and the others leaned forward. "He is driving up from the city and might be home now. The girl friend? I just hear about her." She answered.

Tony collected the empty plastic food plates and disposed of them. "Hey! An important subject change. Where are we all going for spring break? Any one made any plans?"

"You are a senior and had your spring break last year." Victoria Morales said, getting up from the table. "This is our turn. Any one seen the new cool Hunger Game flick?"

"Hey, guys. I am not interfering, but wherever Nancy goes, I plan to go also." Tony said, looking to Nancy for an answer that was not forthcoming. She had great concerns over the implications of what she chose to write in her essay and how her decision might affect her friendships. What else was there for a junior teenage girl, but affection and acceptance from her peers?

Sasha collected her backpack from under the table. "Twenty-one days is no time at all. I made a list. Sort of a division of labor. It consists of all of the questionable successes Obama and the democrats persistently evoke, and all of the negatives provided by the Republicans." She pulled out a legal pad and distributed pages she had torn from it. "It also suggests assignments relative to our quest that deal with information about the president's past, he has refused to release. Additionally, I have included a list of books, that are available in the Library in Woodstock, and I have many to lend. I did check our school library, and most of what we need is well, unavailable. I plan to provide similar resources to the whole class."

"Aren't you the least bit concerned that Ms. Jones will find out about this?" Nancy asked.

Sasha smiled. "After all it would just be rumor, sort of like a Jay Carney answer to anything the more conservative members of the White House press corps ask. She can't do anything until she sees our essays." She looked out the nearby window. "The busses are here. I'd like to come home with you Jillian and see your brother and his new friend. If that's okay with you."

THREE

A Physician's Perspective

When the bus dropped them off, they found her brother, Mark, relaxing in his father's soft recliner, watching the third round of a Florida golf tournament on the Golf Channel. He hit the mute button on the remote, and after hugs and kisses the girls wanted to know where his new 'squeeze' was.

"Karen and Mom took the doggies for a walk up and around the Byrdcliff, " he explained. "They just left so I guess they will be awhile. Amazing that the Aussies took to her immediately. I had my concerns."

"Tell us about her, Mark." Sasha blurted out. She had a crush on him since grade school. "Is this the real thing?"

He smiled. "Well. She certainly is the real thing, but if you are asking me about a more permanent relationship, you will have to wait with the rest of us."

"So what does she look like? What does she like to do for fun, and will she like us?" Jillian said.

"What is not to like about you?" He laughed. "So many questions. Karen is a social worker at Jacobi." He looked at Sasha. "That is where I am doing my residency and that is where I met her. We had a patient in common."

"I want to be a pediatrician, so I want to know everything about everything." Sasha replied excitedly. "Jillian, perhaps we should tell your brother about our assignment. As a doctor, he might have and interesting perspective about obamacare."

"Leave it alone, Sasha. After all he just got here. Besides I want to know more about Karen." Jillian said impatiently.

Mark smiled. "In due time, she will tell you, well, just about everything you should know. So, tell me about the assignment. For what course is it?"

Sasha told him about the Current History class, the teacher and the assignment, as Jillian tried to tone down the rhetoric.

"Look Sash, I agreed to be open minded about all of this. What's new in the City, Mark?" She asked.

"Not much since I am on call twenty four hours and off twelve leaving little time for a social life, let alone going downtown, although we try to take in a museum or a show infrequently as it is." He answered. "I would like to hear more about this essay you all have to write."

Sasha explained further and briefly told him about the late night conversation she had with Jillian. "Although, there is a lot of information to snake through, your sister agreed to take on obamacare first since she really believes it to be a good thing."

Mark thought for a moment. "Jillian. I can provide you with a truthful evaluation of what I see daily at the hospital. I have also read 99 percent of the law, and some of the volumes of regulations produced. Keeping up will be difficult, because they are ever changing. Add to that the frequent and questionable alterations of convenience Obama has made and continues to make. Actually whether or not what he has done is Constitutional, is currently under review in a congressional hearing. So, my Sister, I cannot provide you with an unbiased view, but certainly one that is filled with truths and not lies. I assert that those with an opposite view will not offer the same"

Jillian rocked on her heels. "Well, I promised Dad to look at everything, and he said no matter what, he would support us if and when the shit hit the fan. Well he didn't exactly phrase it that way. It will take Mom and Karen about another forty-five minutes to do the circuit, so you have my undivided attention. Our undivided attention." She looked at Sasha who had not taken her eyes from Mark. "But before you do. What is Karen's position on this?"

"Karen is her own person, but brought up in a family who have voted democratic for as long as she recalls, no matter who the candidate. It is both a problem for her and in some ways a comfort since she is a social worker and looks out for the welfare of her clients. Karen is torn between what is truth and what is fiction, hoping that Obama's Hope and Change was real. She is an idealist. Try not to engage her to strongly about her views about Obama." He looked at Sasha.

"I think that speaking to someone, not involved with school who may have views I might like, would be a good thing." Jillian responded. "We still have time so, give me what you got."

They went to the table with Mark suggesting they take notes. Jillian found a fresh legal pad in her father's study. "Both you and Karen are idealists, which is fine, but we do argue often enough. She doesn't understand when I scream at the television when Obama is giving yet another and "clearer explanation" of his goals. I, on the other hand see no virtue in watching people like Chris Matthews, but I endure it to be fair."

Mark went to the fridge to get another beer, after asking the girls if they wanted something to drink. Both declined. "Okay," he said when he returned.

"Before I say anything else I must tell you both that obamacare or the Affordable Healthcare whatever Law, has absolutely nothing to do with health. It has all to do with power, keeping democrats in office by any means, and forcing socialized medicine by virtue of a one-payer system down the throats of the American people. That is his intent in a nutshell. Whether the Democratic Party really believes in all of this crap is up for grabs." Jillian wrote down what he said using bullet form. Sasha just sat back mesmerized, but she did not learn anything new at this point.

He took a swig of beer. "The law has been fraught with problems since the democratic House of Representatives passed it without one Republican vote. None of those who passed this abomination have admitted that they ever read it. Lobbyists and bureaucrats, with no medical backgrounds, apparently wrote it. Voting on a bill that would impact on one-sixth of the American economy, without reading it and understanding all of its ramifications, should be considered criminal. Voting on any bill without reading it should be reason for recall. When Nancy Pelosi uttered that iconic note of 'wisdom'… 'If we pass it, you will know what's in it'. That goes for her as well."

Sasha asked a question to which she knew the answer. "Mark, why didn't the Republicans offer an alternative bill? I can understand them being in the minority then but since 2010 they have held the majority in the House."

"Actually, they have offered many alternatives that were rejected. Even if a new bill were passed, it would be either rejected by the Senate where the Dems are in the majority, or vetoed by Obama. Harry Reid who considers the Senate his own personal fiefdom places the majority of bills that the House sends to the Senate in the trash. This is the version of justice and democracy used by the Obama administration. Any questions so far?"

Jillian sat with her mouth open. Her pen could not keep up with her brother's explosive explanation. "Not as yet, other than how do I prove what you say?"

"It is part of history. There is plenty of information on the Internet, and the Congressional record is available to all. Watch Fox for un-tampered re-runs of Obama's speeches and promises. They speak for themselves without the need of such as Fact Check or even Snopes whose objectivity I am not certain of. You will not find any mention of anyone holding Obama or the administration responsible for anything that might be construed as harmful, on any of the liberal news networks or in partisan newspapers."

Jillian smiled. "Well I made a deal to watch all of that stuff, so I should be able to form some opinion."

Mark looked at his watch. "Let me fast forward on this. Obama has continually made promises, emphatically stating that with obamacare, everyone could keep their healthcare if they liked it, and their doctors if they liked them, knowing back in 2010 that none of it was true. To date, Jillian, five million Americans have lost their health insurance, cancelled by their insurance companies. This could translate to 15 million just assuming there is a minimum of three people in a family. He lied about all of this in recorded speeches, but has tried to parse his words in an attempt to weasel out of the obvious. There's more. He promised that insurance rates would drop by $2500 per family. They have risen, in some cases up 80% or more. Democrats have ridiculed Sarah Palin for her statement that the law did indeed provide for a Death Panel. Call it what you will, Obama appointed fifteen bureaucrats to make life or death decisions regarding the delivery of services and health care based upon what they deem cost effective, and they answer to no one, and I believe it is a life time appointment. How about them apples?"

Sasha smiled. Jillian put down her pen. "Is there more?" She asked.

Mark finished his beer. "They had three years to develop, complete, and test the website that was to provide access to obamacare. Despite warnings not to do so, they opened it up October 1, and it failed miserably. All kinds of excuses, with the exception of 'my dog ate my software' were offered at Congressional hearings, where these miscreants, including the head of HHS clearly misled the committee of Republicans. The democrats on the committee made every effort to obstruct the flow of information. In criminal law, such is known as 'aiding and abetting'. Now Obama and his cronies are making every effort to have the American public forget by tossing in such red herring as a naïve anti-nuclear proliferation pact with Iran or quick fix immigration reform. No matter how much they protest or cheer it remains a mess. Jillian, the problem is not just the website. It is the entire friggin law. But since I hear the Aussies, let's save more for another time. Girls, this is just the tip of the iceberg. Not Al Gore's iceberg. He is another story and quite a piece of..uh work."

FOUR

Karen

Both Sasha and Jillian liked Karen immediately. Her smile and soft demeanor won them over, and the fact that she clearly loved the Aussies, who allowed her to put her arms around them without any sign of aggressive behavior made Mark and Jennie smile.

"They all love you, Karen. I just know it." Jillian said with tears forming on her cheeks. "I can well understand why Mark loves you, and I can assure you, Daddy will as well."

Mark and Karen both blushed a brilliant crimson while Jennie smiled broadly. Sasha frowned, because in the forty-five minutes spent with Mark, she was again infatuated with him, the first time having occurred when he was eighteen and she attended Jillian's eighth birthday party. She admired Karen, but did some quick math coming to the conclusion that when he was thirty and she, twenty, a relationship was certainly a possibility.

Sasha wanted to get Karen alone, and suggested that she and Jillian and Karen go for a short walk. As they were about to leave, Stanley Ashton arrived and met Karen.

"Jennie, did you have any thoughts about dinner?" He asked.

"We have so much in the freezer, nothing would be a problem." She responded, taking his jacket, laying it over a chair.

"Tell you what I think." He said. "With Karen and Mark home, a rarity, but home, nevertheless, I am going to call the restaurant up at Rip Van Winkle Golf Course and reserve a table for 7 pm. The food actually rivals that of the best Woodstock has to offer, and the young couple that own it John and Sara are really nice people."

"But we belong to Wiltwyk and know so many of the people." Jennie protested.

"Less pretentious at RVP. I played there last week and I think you might like to play there as well, Jen. I just feel so comfortable there."

"Look, Dad," Mark interjected. "You will get no argument from us." He looked at Karen who nodded. "And Sasha must go as well. I know Palenville, so we can take her home right down 32 into Saugerties. It will be a piece of cake."

Sasha eagerly agreed. "I'll call my folks right now. With tomorrow being Saturday, it is not a problem."

Jillian looked at her quizzically. "Sasha, what about Shabbat?

Jennie saw the discomfort in Sasha's eyes. "I shall call your Mom and tell her that we are taking you out with the family for a very special occasion and that if it really was late, you would stay the night with us."

Without thinking, Mark said. "And I could drive you home tomorrow." He squeezed Karen's hand.

Sasha smiled. "I am absolutely certain that it will be okay with my folks for me to stay over."

Sasha's mother and father were pleased that she was with people she considered family and that was enough for them. While they observed dietary rules at home, they understood there were times where they could not control the place or the fare offered to their daughter. This applied particularly to a daughter growing up in a far different world that either of them had ever known.

The drive to Palenville and the restaurant was actually quite short in time, with Stanley having learned of a more direct route, consisting of a left and a right turn after leaving the West Saugerties road. The restaurant was busy so making reservations proved to be a plus. After they were seated, Stanley ordered a Manhattan and Mark followed suit. Karen and Jennie selected ice teas while the young girls opted for colas. After an order of fried calamari for the table had been consumed, Stanley chose Lobster tails, Mark, surf and turf, Karen and Jennie the grilled Salmon while the girls decided to share an order of macaroni and cheese, not on the menu but, available. Finally sated, no one wanted to look at the dessert menu. Jillian said that Sasha would stay the night since they had lots of stuff to talk about.

Around 11:30, Sasha came down to get a drink of water and found Stanley and Mark watching re-runs of earlier Fox Channel programs.

"I thought I heard some chatter down here." She said.

"Probably me cursing out one of the liberal talking heads in disguise as news contributors." Mark replied.

"What's going on down here?" Jillian asked as she came down from her bedroom.

"Stuart Varney just interviewed Ezekiel Emmanuel. Well actually, Varney asked questions and that putz Ezekiel provided no answers." Stanley said.

"Where is Karen?" Sasha asked.

"Said she was tired so she went to bed." Mark said.

"Mom as well." Stanley offered.

"So, I heard you yelling at something Mark. You two having and argument?" Jillian asked.

"Not likely," Stanley responded. "Varney asked Ezekiel if he would put his own personal information into the obamacare website and to look at the camera and assure America that it was safe to do so. He actually refused."

"Who is this guy?" Jillian asked.

"He is one of dregs that drew up obamacare." Sasha said.

"How do you know all this?" Jillian sked.

"I just make a point to know about everything I think might be important, and my folks discuss stuff like this all the time." Sasha answered. This guy, Emmanuel is a brother of the current Chicago mayor, and if you watch the news, at least someone seems to be murdered on a daily basis in that city. Any way, this guy is supposed to be a medical doctor, He has made comments that would suggest he strongly favors euthanasia."

Jillian went into the kitchen and returned with two glasses of lemonade. "I'm really tired." She handed Sasha a glass and went back up stairs to her room. "See you all in the morning."

Sasha looked at Mark. "She should be the one to stay and listen. What other awful things is our government doing?"

Stanley frowned. "Well, back in September the untersturmfuhrer of the Senate, Reid said that his staff would not be exempt from participating in obamacare. Today he exempted them."

"That's not legal. Is it?" Sasha asked.

"Is anything this government does really legal?" Mark replied. "Congress passes laws that infringe upon the rights of all Americans, and then weasels out by subterfuge to exempt themselves from that law they passed."

"What is Karen's take on all this?" Stanley asked.

Mark sighed. "Karen comes from a very liberal background, and it goes far back. Her family truly seems to have been born democrats and filled with some bizarre form of guilt. They fight for every cause, whether right or wrong, and support some of the worst criminals in politics just because they belong to the Democratic Party."

"And Karen goes along with all of this?" Sashay asked.

"Karen is troubled by some of it, but has difficulty admitting her doubts. It is as if she is in a state of denial which provides her a sheltered comfort zone from the truth." Mark answered sadly.

"I see that this makes you very unhappy." Sasha said. "Do you fight a lot over this?"

Stanley squirmed in his chair, as Mark's face reddened. "We have many discussions that may not end too well. I think it's time for me to retire." Mark said as a got up. "Goodnight. See you all in the morning." He then made his way to his bedroom and quietly closed the door.

Stanley had remained seated. "So, Sasha, what's going on with you and these questions?"

"I am so turned on by politics and issues that involve medicine, since that will be my future. Did I ask a bad question?" Sasha yawned.

"I think that it best not to push too hard. Mark and Karen should be able to work out all issues, no matter how difficult by themselves. Now, time for all of us to retire. What are your plans for tomorrow? Going home?" He asked as he started for the master bedroom.

"I would like to hang around with you guys if you don't mind that is. And thank you so much for your hospitality and of course dinner." Sasha said, smiling sweetly, as she went up the stairs to join Jillian, whom she hoped was still awake.

"Jillian. You up?" Got some gossip." Sasha said as she crawled into the bed.

Jillian rolled over onto her stomach and covered her ears with her hands. "Go to sleep. I don't want to hear anymore about our government." She said.

"You mean you're not convinced yet? Unbelievable, but that's not what I've got." Sasha responded turning out the light on the night table. "I think your brother and Karen have major problems, and all because of their political views."

"Then please do not fan the fires if they are lit. Go to sleep!" Jillian pleaded.

"Okay," Sasha responded, "but here is some stuff I want in your head to perhaps dream about. Because, in the next few days, you will have to deal with all of them, if you plan to write an honest essay. Ready or not. Fast and Furious. Benghazi, Muslim Brotherhood, NSA, IRS and of course the ever unpopular obamacare. These are just a few of the scandals that we all know about, and that Obama and his crew deny exist. Oh, we also have to take on his birth certificate and such. Read Corsi's book."

FIVE

Bubbles Bursting

Jennie opened the door to Jillian's room, and looked inside. Both girls appeared to be still sound asleep, but Jillian turned and looked at the digital clock on her night table. Then she saw her mother approach.

"High Mom. Good morning" She yawned and stretched. "Clock says 9 a.m. That can't be right."

"It's right. Sorry to disturb you." She whispered so as to not awaken Sasha. "You have a call downstairs from one of your friends at school. She said it was about school and important. Should I have her call back or take her number?"

"No. Just want to wash my face and brush my teeth. Tell her I'll be a minute or so." Jillian said as she stretched, got out of bed, and padded her way to the bathroom.

Jillian, still in her pajamas, came into the kitchen and picked up the phone. Kelly Storey, the only African-American student in her class, was on the other end. Kelly had been a close friend since third grade when her family moved from Montgomery Alabama to Shady, considered part of Woodstock. Her father, Malcolm was a neurologist at the hospital in Kingston, and one of Stanley's golfing buddies. Stanley knew Malcolm had voted for Obama at least once, since Malcolm told him he had.

"Morning Kell. What's up?" Jillian asked, as Sasha came into the kitchen, and accepted a glass of orange juice offered by Jennie. I am in the kitchen with my Mom and Sasha. Is this something private?"

"Not exactly, but sort of. Maybe I should call back at a better time." Kelly said.

"Tell you what. Give me a half hour to grab some breakfast and shower and I'll call you back on your cell." Jillian said, as Sasha raised her eyebrows.

"Deal. I'll wait for your call." Kelly responded, and the line went dead.

Karen came into the kitchen and said that Mark had left to play a round of golf with Stanley. "I forget to mention that," Jennie remarked. "Stanley said that the weather was unusually warm for this time of year, but he would be good for nine holes only."

Sasha offered to take the dogs for a walk and Karen said the four could be too much for her alone, so she would be happy to join her. Jennie told them that she had some washing to do so they should go ahead without her.

Once outside, Sasha held the leads attached to Shane and Kodi, and Karen had control of Shelby and Ranger, both of whom tried to decide the route to take.

"These two wish to go up through the woods, but the road seems to end up there." Karen said.

"Not a problem," Sasha answered as her two dogs pulled ahead of the others. "There is some underbrush, but your boots will do just fine. This will take us up to the Upper Byrdcliff, and there we can make a decision to turn right or left. Each way will go downhill eventually."

When they reached the Upper Byrdcliff, all four dogs pulled to the left. "I guess they want to pass the old Whitehead Place. Up here is where the Art Colony was first founded. If our guys here had selected a right turn we would have come to a sign at the base of the hill that explains all about it."

The silence of the crisp morning was periodically broken by the call of some blue jays sitting high in trees whose foliage had already began to turn red and orange.

"Autumn is beautiful up here." Karen said. "Don't you think?"

"You sort of get used to it. Living up here I guess. One of my friends is a landscape artist. Takes some courses in the Woodstock School of Art. For him it is an artists candy land or so he says."

"Where do you live Sasha?" Karen asked as Shelby stopped to smell the base of a tree.

"Saugerties. About eight miles east. Bigger town than Woodstock. More stuff to see and do. But Woodstock is just unique." Sasha responded.

"You are Jewish. I gathered that when you spoke about your parents honoring the Sabbath. Were you bat mitzvah?"

"Of course, and not that long ago," Sasha said shyly. "Where are you from Karen?"

"I was brought up in Brooklyn. My grandparents emigrated to America and chose Brooklyn because their friends had." Karen said.

"And you are Jewish as well? Were you bat mitzvah as well?" Sasha asked.

"My family is Jewish. My grandparents were born to Jews who lived forever, apparently in Poland. They are all gone now." Karen responded sadly. "I was not bat mitzvah."

"What happened to them?" Sasha asked, and then sighed."Oh, my. The Holocaust. My folks took me to the museum in Washington."

"I have been there as well," Karen said, as the dogs began to pick up the pace. "As little that they speak of it, my grandparents say that if one was not there, to experience the horror, the museums only can tell but a small part of the story."

"I cannot imagine. My father is a third generation American. My great-great grandmother used to tell them stories about the terrible pogroms in Kiev. She was one of the lucky ones being hidden by gentiles in their root cellars." Sasha said and added, "My stepmother came as an immigrant."

Karen smiled. "Ah, then we have something in common, Sasha. My grandparents knew each other from a small town just outside of Warsaw. When the Nazis came and all of the Jews were forced into the ghetto, Christians took them in and hid them for the duration of the war. One day after the war was over, and when the Russians weren't looking, they were brought to a Red Cross unit. They were both nineteen at the time. Ultimately, they learned that everyone had perished in the camps."

"Then what happened?" Sasha asked.

"They made enough money to come to the United States, passed through Ellis Island, found Brooklyn, and thought it was the natural thing for them to marry." Karen continued. They had four children. My Dad, his brother and two younger sisters. They all married and had families of their own. Dad met Mom at one of those dance studios in Manhattan, and six months later got married."

"Why weren't you bat mitzvah then?" Sasha inquired.

"My grandparents did not believe in God, because they all had been forsaken. They had this tremendous amount of guilt that for some reason, they, and no other member of the family survived."

"They would not go to the museum in Washington with us because, grandfather said he had been there already in real time. My mother came from a conservative Jewish family in New Jersey, but loved my Father and my grandparent too much to do anything that might upset them. Her only family is my aunt since both grandparents on her side are deceased." Karen said, as they finally reached the Glasco turnpike.

Karen stopped and both Shelby and Ranger sat by her side. "I regret not being bat mitzvah, but I guess I always could if I so chose."

"Do you or they lean politically one way or the other? My folks have considered themselves Independents, and have so for a while now." Sasha probed.

Karen though about how she would answer for a moment. "They were young during Franklin Roosevelt's presidency, so they, like so many Jews were democrats, and voted party line no matter what. Intellectual? No, but very stubborn. At least that is what my father tells me. Did they have a false belief in Roosevelt?" Her voice changed to a whisper. "Between you and me I believe he was an anti-Semite. It was natural living in Bed Sty, that my grandparents were easily swayed by Socialism. My great uncle, Charlie was a movie producer in Hollywood during the McCarthy era, so from that time on, with the exception of a few relatives, they all hate Republicans."

"Are you a Socialist, Karen?" Sasha's voice trembled.

"Perhaps in some respect, but I still believe in capitalism, free enterprise and certainly the Constitution. But I am disturbed by the inequality that dictates who have health care and who do not. Mark and I argue constantly about that and certainly about Obama. I voted twice for him. What I have not told Mark is that I have some regrets." Karen said tearfully.

"Why not just tell him?" Sasha asked.

"Oh he would probably lord it over me. We have gone through similar issues, so I know his game plan." Karen responded.

"Do you love Mark?" Sasha finally asked.

"Oh, yes, so very much." Karen responded as they continued to walk.

"And, Mark. Does he love you?" Sasha persisted.

"I think he does. He says he does, but some time I wonder." Karen said.

"Is he good doctor?" Sasha asked.

"Mark is a wonderful doctor." Karen said with a broad smile.

"I plan to be a pediatrician. I really must start to look at colleges and Universities." Sasha said.

"I attended NYU, and got a great education. Enough to land the job that I wanted at Bronx Muncipal." Karen said.

"And then you met Mark." Sasha said.

"And then I met Mark." Karen responded. "We are back at the house. Jennie said we should take off their leads after we get them in the gate. They can do what ever business they missed." The dogs took off after some imaginary something as they chased down to the end of the enclosed property, barking all the way.

"Karen, our class has been given a topic for an essay which could as my brother would say, turn out to be a real hot potato. It is politically charged, and could be a factor in our grades and futures. I am certain that Jillian would agree you would be a big help with it." Sasha said.

Karen stopped at the front door and turned to Sasha. "I would love to help you if I can. When is this due?"

Sasha told her that they had barely twenty days.

"Okay, I am not certain what Mark or you folks have planned for today and tomorrow. We leave tomorrow, so let's find the time. Also remind me to give you my email address and there is always that thing called a phone." Karen laughed. She seemed to be relieved of a great burden.

SIX

Revelation

When Karen and Sasha finally collected the dogs that were rooting around the pear tree for the last of the fruit that might still be lying on the ground, let them into the house, and found Jennie putting some scones in the oven. Jennie told Sasha that Jillian was on the phone up in her room and offered Karen a cup of green tea that she had just brewed.

Jennie brought the tea into the living room and the two sat down on the sofa, near the woodstove whose dull embers were just showing signs of coming to life.

"So, Karen." Jennie sad with a glint in her eyes, "may I ask you? What are your intentions?"

Karen began to laugh hysterically. "Isn't that what the girl's father supposed to ask the boy?" She could hardly get the words out. Then after composing herself, she took Jennie's hand in hers. "If I knew, I certainly would tell you."

Jennie laughed. "I was kidding."

Karen drank some tea and then leaned her head back on the couch. "We met six months ago. I went to the ward to check on a patient and Mark, I found out was his assigned physician. Some of the new residents have uncompromising egos and they get into a turf battle with the likes of the lowly social worker. Mark could not have been more helpful. I saw him a few times, again at the bed site, and one afternoon, when I went to the hospital cafeteria, there he was amidst a bevy of fawning first and second year nursing students. He saw me sit down, excused himself, asked if he could join me, and we have been together, on and off since then.

Jennie looked perplexed. "Why on and off? If I may ask."

"Of course." Karen thought for a moment. "As much as we are similar and like so many of the same things, we are so very different. He has never yet asked to meet my family, but that could be because I have scared him off with my anecdotes. I never asked him his religion and he never offered it. The surname did not sound Jewish, but I would have no problem in any event."

Jennie smiled. "Mark was raised Jewish although other than his bar mitzvah, one would never know it. Because of me, I am Jewish. Stanley sometimes might attend a service for a major holiday with us, but just to be accommodating. So, that's that. You never explained on and off."

"Okay. Mark's political views are different than mine. He is very conservative and will vote Republican and I was 'born' into the Democratic Party and never left. I voted for Obama twice, but have now, reservations. You might call me a Progressive who believes in some strange way that capitalism is good, entrepreneurs are needed and following the laws of our Constitution vital. Then the social worker in me wakes up and I feel for the common man, the needy, the hungry and the homeless." Karen looked to Jennie for a response.

"Why Karen, everything you say is commendable. What on earth is the problem with my son? Jennie said. "More tea?"

"Still have some, Jennie. I have the same problem with my family. Getting them together for any holiday, a celebration or a death, generally leads to a melee between the Republican side and the Democratic side of the family. Grandma's solution, when she sees it coming is to get out the cards, and the poker chips and set up a game of penny poker so they can vent their aggressions with innuendo and not their fists."

"I must tell you, if you have not already noticed, that this family is very conservative in its views, well, except for Jillian, who still has to grow up a bit. Obama has done more to create a schism between us and many of our friends who see liberalism, big government and spending as the great panacea. Stanley will not go to dinner with any of them, not because there might be an altercation, but because he cannot believe that they believe everything the man says, and will not even consider that his policies might be ruining the country. It is this narrow-minded attitude, that he will not abide."

"I truly believe Mark sees me like that and I am not like that. No one is infallible; least of all the president who has less than a 40% approval rate, or a Congress whose approval rate is deep down in single digits. I get it. I really get. Mark does not get that I get it, however. There in lies the off and on." Karen said.

"Perhaps, then both of you should try to maintain more of a neutral posture politically. Personally, I don't see where your views are so out of line. Try not to discuss politics until Obama and his gang are gone. After all, the majority of happy marriages, that were meant to be outlast politicians and the good and the bad they do. Go to dinner and just eat dinner. Go on a vacation and talk about the future. Never run for political office. If that Matalin woman and her strange looking husband from Louisiana can do it, anyone can. I don't agree with everything Stanley says, just most of it." Jennie laughed.

SEVEN

Explanation

Sasha opened the door to Jillian's room and found her deep in conversation on her cell phone. She started to speak when Jillian turned, indicated that she close the door and signed that she should be quiet. Sasha sat down on the bed as Jillian activated the speaker on her phone.

"Kelly, Sasha just came in and I turned on the speaker. If you want me to turn it off I will, and I'll ask her to leave." Jillian said.

Kelly's voice came over sharp and clearly. "That's fine. After all this is a school assignment we must deal with. Sasha may listen in."

"Let's catch her up. Sasha, Kelly is very concerned about the consequences that might develop as a result of our not completing the assignment that way Ms. Jones or perhaps the school wishes us to do so. Okay, Kell, what do want to share?" Jillian said.

"I should provide some background first. Well, before we all were born, my folks lived in Montgomery, Alabama, right at the beginning of the Civil Rights movement. These were tough times for Dad as well even as a young boy. Schools were segregated, restaurants were segregated, and water fountains were segregated. Black baseball players could not stay with the team even after Jackie Robinson, for a long time. My grandfather marched at Selma, and you know from what we have learned how terrible that was." Kelly said.

"I just cannot imagine," Sasha remarked. "How terrible things were for African-Americans."

"Perhaps I should clarify one point before I go any further." Kelly said. "My Dad, long ago, told me that he does not consider himself African-American. He said he and the rest of the Storey's are American first as far back as he can remember or was ever told. He gets very incensed when he hears it and says that political correctness has done more to harm race relations than anything, well except for the efforts put forth by the president."

"Got it." Jillian said. "Go on, please."

"Blacks have had very few heroes. Among them were Jack Kennedy, his brother, Robert and Martin Luther King, all of whom had their young lives cut short. So who followed? Baseball players, boxers and then rappers, many of who were terrible role providers. Then suddenly, we had Barack Obama. You can readily understand how his presence made us feel so invigorated. He spoke so well and said all of the right things we wanted to hear. There was something akin to a hypnotic spell that most of America, black and white was under, that we did not comprehend everything he really said, and what his true agenda might have been. So Hope and Change was great PR. His use of the Internet to spread his message among the young and naïve, who voted for him, was a work of genius. My Dad, an educated man and a physician, bought it hook, line and sinker, at least in November of 2008. He did not vote for him in 2012, since Obama's direction toward socialism had become obvious, well, at least to Dad."

"Okay." Kelly took a breath. "Dad read a good part of the Healthcare act when it was still a bill. He saw, apparently, what few people saw and realized how it would destroy the best health care in the world. Uh, Jillian. Your brother is a resident. He must have shared something."

"Mark has told me most of what he considers bad. But I still think it might be best to work out the glitches and see what shakes out." Jillian responded.

"Actually, he told us about a lot of people losing their health care completely, and now they are scrambling to find new plans before the deadline." Sasha said.

"And the Democrats have minimized the number of cancellations, none of which would happen despite Obama promises. Period! You guys know Harvey Allen? He had to go back into public school because of financial issues? Well, his Dad lost his job and has not been able to find a new one. Ellen, his sister, who was diagnosed with leukemia, now is in remission, because of her doctors and hospital. Well. His health insurance, that he obviously liked, was cancelled. He has no idea if her doctors or hospital will be in any plan and neither do they. He did look into newer plans, but the deductibles start at $6500 and his premiums each month will more than double. This is one story of thousands, and not just made up anecdotal reprisals by democrats." Kelly said.

"That is terrible." Both Sasha and Jillian said in unison.

"It does not end there. Fifty colleagues, physicians, my father knows in Connecticut have been dropped by the companies whose insured they have provided care for, and were terminated without explanation. Dad says it is just to reduce costs, by limiting visits and services to patients by having fewer providers in the system to pay. As it is doctors in Medicare get maybe, 70 cents on the dollar and if Congress, in the limited time left to play the game "lawmaker" don't act, it will be reduced by another 27%." Kelly continued.

"Why would Obama want to destroy our health care system?" Jillian asked.

Sasha grimaced. "The plan has always been to have a one payer system. Add to that his power grab, and the disgusting push of Democrats to remain in office forever. And no one loses their job, no matter who dies, no matter how much fraud, or how many lies are told."

"Dad said the same thing. Obama wants to socialize medicine. Dad calls him names I cannot repeat, and some of them are, well, just take it at that." Kelly responded.

"Mark did say most of those things." Jillian said. "So, who are your heroes, Kell?"

"Dad said that he liked Colin Powell until he became," Her voiced was reduced to a whisper. "An Uncle Tom. You know." She thought for a moment. "Alan West, a former Congressman from Florida, would be a great example of a hero. He was former military and elected in 2010, but lost in 2012. Dad says it was because the democrats gerrymandered his district, among other things. He likes Dr. Ben Carson, and believes he has a great future beyond medicine. He believes some of the congressmen and women from New York and California are self-serving racists, interested only in how they can improve their own financial lot. Heroes are few and far between, at least from the ranks of black Americas."

"I am getting a picture, I don't like." Jillian said. "I can understand your concerns about the essay. If we write a negative one there will be hell to pay."

"Now is the time to get everyone on the same page," Sasha said. "Karen said she would help if she could. "We have to figure out a way to tell the truth, and do it in a manner not to jeopardize our futures."

"Sounds like a tall order to me." Kelly said.

"No kidding, and we only have touched the tip of the ice berg. Sorry, I forgot, Al Gore said it was melting. We still have to deal with Fast and Furious, IRS. NSA, Benghazi, Solyndra, Windmills, Gas prices, Taxes, and assorted other scandals and lies. Kell you still there?"

"I'm listening. Oh, I forgot to tell you that the group of so called or alleged white coated doctors who stood behind Obama when he was touting his health care plan, were issued their white coats and stethoscopes by central casting's wardrobe mistress."

"Sounds about right to me." Sasha said. They went through a list of their classmate names and arranged to call them in the afternoon.

EIGHT

Fore Play

Stanley and Mark practiced on the putting green of the Woodstock Golf Club, as they waited for Malcolm Storey and Ralph Cummins to complete their foursome. The elder Ashton has just sunk a fifteen-foot putt when he heard a green Kia Sorrento roar into the parking lot. He was taken aback when he did not see Ralph with Malcolm, but someone he didn't know. Quick introductions were made, so they would not forfeit their tee time, and then Malcolm and Stanley went into the small clubhouse to sign in and pay for their guests.

"Who is this guy," Stanley inquired. "What happened to Ralph?"

"He was called into the hardware store. They were short help, so it is livelihood. Anyhow, Bob Fellnick is his brother-in-law. Ralph really didn't offer to have him join us, but he was overly insistent. Look, we have two hours with this guy. I warn you. Do not talk politics. During the ten minute drive here, I learned quickly, he was a flaming liberal."

"Great. If he falls into the pond on 5, we look the other way." Stanley said. "What does he do?"

"Been in the school system in the City for years, and now has some plushy union job as well. You better warn Mark early so he doesn't get into it with him." Malcolm said.

They caught up with Bob and Mark, who were walking across the narrow wooden bridge that led to the first tee. "Catch up to Mark. I have to get a pull cart for Bob." Malcolm advised.

They gave Bob Felnick the honors. Mark stood behind him, and suggested that if he had a tendency to slice, better to aim more to the left side of the fairway.

"Son, I was playing golf when you were still in diapers." Bob said. After about ten practice swings, he sliced the ball into Rt. 375 and into on coming traffic.

"You got good homeowners insurance there Bob?" Stanley called out, as Felnick drove his second ball about 100 yards into the rough on the left side as he over compensated.

Bob took a mulligan, and then watched the other three drive their balls into the center of the fairway with Mark's flying a good ten yards beyond the others. Mark birdied the first hole and both Malcolm and Stanley bogied it. The other three never saw what Felnick had put down on his scorecard. The latter's game seemed to improve a bit over the next two holes. However, when he attempted to chip to the green on the third hole, he over shot it by ten yards.

As Stanley was lining up his putt, Felnick distracted him. "What do you docs think of the new health care law?"

"Can't you see I am about to sink a crucial putt?" Stanley said angrily.

"Sorry," Felnick said, turning to Mark. "How about you?"

As Stanley's ball stopped about a foot passed the hole, Felnick muttered. "Bad luck."

Mark made par, sinking a ten-foot putt and turned to Felnick. "It is really bad sport to talk when someone is putting. Sort of screws up ones concentration. And you question about obamacare, it sucks just like its author and namesake!"

Felnick walked up to the 4th tee even though he did not have the honors. "Hmmm. Water ahead. 175 to the flag," he read off the sign. He teed up the ball and swung. The ball was more of a low line drive that hit the sprinkler that lay in the middle of the pond and bounced hard enough to reach the dry land ten feet from the small, circular green. "Just as I played it." He smirked.

Stanley decided not to tee up and chose a seven iron. With a smooth swing and proven finish, the ball landed five feet from the pin. Malcolm landed his ball between Stanley's and the flag.

It was Mark's turn. Stronger and younger than the others, he picked up a pitching wedge, and lofted the ball high in the air, landing it softly on the small incline a foot behind the hole.

"You are too young and too smart to be one of those racists, so I hope you are not against the healthcare bill cause he is black." Felnick said as they caught up to Malcolm and Stanley.

"Hey! Bob." Malcolm said emphasizing the last letter. "You happen to notice that I am black? So if you want to call it an early game, keep on talking."

The par 5, fifth tee box, looked out on a long curving fairway that slightly doglegged to the left. Felnick managed a decent drive that landed in the fairway on the right side. Again all three of the others sent their drives well over 200 yards, where they had a straight approach to the green that lay just beyond a small pond. Felnick's second shot landed in high grass again off to the right of the fairway. Mark offered to help find it. After a few minutes of waiting, Stanley and Malcolm came over to help.

"Five minute rule for lost ball. He's got two minutes left." Stanley said. "Hey, Mark, you still looking for his ball?"

"Actually, no," Mark said with a wry smile. "It is under my right foot."

Malcolm laughed. "Damn shame and quite appropriate. Thank God they only package three balls to a box. That leaves one left." They mentioned the five-minute rule so Felnick tossed a ball into the middle of the fairway. He still had the honors. This time he drove the ball high in the air but far enough to hit a hill next to the pond causing the ball to roll down the embankment, but not entering the water.

Malcolm and Stanley both left themselves a chip shot to the undulating green, while Mark's ball wound up about four feet from the hole. Felnick was left trying to figure out how to hit his ball without him winding up in the water.

"Never had a lie like this before." He called out.

"Bet you've told a bunch of them." Stanley muttered.

"Patience, Brother, he like the rest of his people know not what they do." Malcolm said.

"We should have decided to have him get dunked on the fourth. This one is far too shallow." Mark said, walking toward the green. Then Felnick miraculously lofted the ball, with his 56' wedge, landing it next to Mark's.

"I think you have been holding out on us Bob. Good thing we're not playing for money." Stanley said as he chipped the ball into the hole for par.

"I doubt you should worry about money, being a doctor and all that." Felnick countered.

"Well your good buddy's idea of fairness and wealth distribution is going destroy American health care, ration services and drive scores of good doctors into early retirement." Stanley checked the distance to he hole with his GPS.

He leaned against the golf cart. "But of course, you being a teacher in the City school system, don't have to worry about your job, because even if you fuck up, your union will find a nice soft rubber room for you to read dirty magazines, while you still collect your pay." Stanley was steaming.

The last four holes were played in relative silence, except for the noise the clubs made as they struck the balls. Malcolm had taken Stanley aside, and told him to cool it, so they stayed together while Mark walked with Bob Felnick. When they had rolled their balls into the cup on the 9th green, they shook hands.

"Hey guys, no hard feelings. I would like to make amends and try to give you my point of view on all this over some single malt." Felnick offered.

"I think not," Malcolm said. "Its only 10:30 a.m. and the bar is closed."

"Thank God," Stanley muttered under his breath. He walked over to Malcolm. "Good luck on the drive back."

"Sorry guys, it couldn't be helped." Malcolm said. Stanley laughed, as Mark and Malcolm shook hands. "Mark, I would like to speak with you about some cases I have some questions about." Mark smiled. He was on cloud nine that a long practicing doctor might seek his counsel.

Stanley and Mark cleaned and bagged their clubs as they watched Malcolm drive off. "Sorry about my outburst. I just had enough of him." Stanley offered.

Mark patted his father on the back. "I thought you were terrific."

NINE

Epiphany

When Stanley opened the front door, there were no dogs to greet them so the house was unusually quiet. Jennie was not in the kitchen, and Mark found no sign of Karen as well.

"They must have taken the dogs for a walk." Mark said, when Sasha and Jillian bounded down the stairs.

"Mom and Karen went shopping." Jillian said. "She left French toast in the microwave and said that the maple syrup is in the fridge. And she brewed a fresh pot of coffee. They will be home around noon."

"Good. I forgot to tell her we are having guests for dinner. I will see if I can get her on her cell." Jennie did not answer her phone, so Mark tried Karen who answered on the first ring when she saw it was Mark calling. Mark gave the phone to Stanley.

"Hi Karen, Jennie with you?" He asked. When Jennie got on the phone, he found out that she had decided to take the doggies to the kennel for an overnight. "Good idea," he said. "We can have some uninterrupted time, since the Aussies will not be in an uproar with each motorcycle, truck or car speeding down past the house." He then proceeded to tell her that he had invited, Pastor Joe from the Lutheran church, Father Anthony from the Catholic church and Rabbi Tom, from the Jewish congregation. Not certain yet if he'll come. It is Saturday, after all."

"I hope the rabbi is not kosher, since there is no fresh fish here. We have chicken in the freezer and I'll get some beef ribs then." Jennie said.

"Rather pork baby backs. We won't discuss the origin. See you in a bit." Stanley said and hit the end button. Mark told him that he got the gist of the conversation.

"When did you invite the clergy, and why?" Mark asked, as he poured himself a glass of orange juice.

"When we stopped for some New York's overpriced gas. When I went in to pay, I had to wait on line anyway, so I made the calls. The rabbi's son said he would have his father call. As to why, I thought their sense of how the administration might be fomenting a form of religious persecution, under the guise of fairness would be worth some discussion."

"Dad you are really excited about this." Mark said.

"I am overjoyed." Stanley replied.

"How do you plan to fit all of this into one day?" Mark asked.

"We are going to do as much as we can today without exhausting everyone's brains, and tackle the rest tomorrow." Stanley said. "Too bad all of your classmates won't be here."

Jillian came in and heard the last part of the conversation. "Mom does not need any more surprises." She said.

Sasha chimed in. "We can catch the rest of the guys up, over the next few days."

An hour later Jennie and Karen arrived with their purchases. "Neat town, I would like to see more of it. They even have flea market." Karen said.

"I was thinking, salads for lunch, so we brought fresh veggies, and we also could have soup if anyone wanted it." Jennie offered.

Sasha piped in. "I'm good for soup."

Stanley laughed and put his arm around her. "Anything your heart desires. You are one of the family, after all."

After a quick lunch, Stanley sat everyone down in the living room. "Want to make sure no one is being imposed upon, so we will not go through the exercise if even one person has an objection for any reason. So I have cut up paper into six small squares. Pencils are on the table so write an N or a Y on the paper and let's see what will we place them in? Ah my nice clean, recently laundered Barbados golf hat." He removed the cap from a hook and placed it on the table, next to the small pieces of paper. Each of them wrote on their papers and placed them in the cap. "Okay, Karen, you mix them around without looking, and then pick them out and tell us the result."

Karen did just as he asked, and smiled." All Ys and nary an N."

"Great!" Stanley said. "Okay. Here on the living room TV we shall have Fox News. Mark. Turn the TV in our bedroom to CNN, and Jillian why don't you put MSNBC on your TV. There will not be any news on the major channels since they will be devoted to college football all afternoon."

The phone rang, just as two members of the clergy knocked on the front door. "It's the rabbi, Jennie said. He's on his way."

A half hour later, the three clerics, and Stanley, and Jennie were seated on sofas while Mark, Karen, and the two young girls sat close by on the carpeted floor. Stanley had muted the sound on the television, but the scroll across the bottom of the screen and the topics being discussed were easily observed. Both Jillian and Sasha took turns explaining the assignment.

"Seems to me that your teacher gave you very little wiggle room to make up your own minds, as to what your conclusion might be." Rabbi Tom Spector noted. He was a tall, bony man, who had been hired to replace the rabbi who had recently retired. The young members of the congregation particularly liked this guitar playing religious leader, who was much closer to their ages than the well-respected octogenarian, who had led services for over thirty years.

Father Anthony Lobato had been the leader of St. Jerome's Catholic church for twenty years. He settled his portly frame back into the soft couch and listened quietly. Pastor Joe Fraizer had recently come from Tucson, Arizona, to be religious leader of a small congregation at Woodstock's Second Lutheran Church. Dressed in blue jeans and a dark grey sweatshirt, one who did not know him, would never take him for a minister.

"So," Pastor Joe observed, "I am certain that you girls have not called upon us for our excellence in economics. How can we be of help to you?"

"Let me answer that for you Pastor." Mark began. "Jillian has decided to tackle the problem from the issue of health care as her main issue, and use some of the others to support whatever premise she decides upon. Do I have that right?"

"I think so." Jillian replied. "There are a number of religious issues that have perplexed me, as well as other members of the class who are not Catholic. Specifically abortion, birth control, and free, well not really free contraception."

"Don't forget the regulations that require insurance companies to provide pediatric dental care and maternity care to people whether they need it or want it, at considerable extra cost." Sasha interjected.

"Seems to me that those are parallel issues. Perhaps Father Anthony would be interested in expressing his views since they do affect Catholics in more ways." Rabbi Tom said.

"And don't forget the fact that liberals and atheists are trying to do away with Christmas and so many holidays that haven't offended me, as a Jew. I rather like Christmas time with the beautiful carols and Easter with the bunny. And don't forget Santa. I heard that Macy's has a Santa who is not allowed to say Merry Christmas. Is that true?" Sasha, out of breath, concluded.

"All right, Sasha, let me see how much of that I can remember." Father Anthony said with a smile, as Jillian asked Sasha in a whisper, where she had heard the Macy story. "I think I can be an expert witness regarding some of the more important things, not to suggest that Santa and the Easter Bunny are, as you say chopped liver."

Observing that he had their complete attention, Father Anthony leaned forward and placing his hands together, tented his fingers. "We all have witnessed the constant bombardment of commercials on television promoting certain drugs, but with major lengthy provisos or disclaimers as well. If you glance at the TV, you will see one right this moment. It seems to me that whatever good the drugs are meant to achieve are rather small compared the terrible side effects that could occur as a result of their use. Why should not politicians, particularly, any seeking the highest office in this country be held to similar standards?" He looked at Jillian and Sasha. "Perhaps they should also have disclaimers."

Jillian raised her hand as if in class. "How might we use this in writing our essays? I decided to start with obamacare?"

"Patience, patience, and you are not in class my dear, so no protocol for hand raising to make a point or ask a question. I will bring together how the health care law might adversely affect the religious principles of many, and also touch upon issues that have a decided impact upon how people interact with each other." Father Anthony said.

He thought for a moment. "Back to the idea of disclaimers, and to your point Jillian as to how to develop it into your assignment. So, since I do not believe this was meant to be a monologue, why doesn't everyone make a contribution? First, as to what is the good?"

Karen was the first to offer her opinion. "He was the first Afro-American to be elected president." Sasha and Jillian immediately recalled what Kelly had said.

"I would agree with that," Rabbi Tom interjected. "The black community suddenly had a lot of pride, that was long coming."

"We need a scribe." Jennie, said. "I volunteer."

"Actually, that should be the girl's job." Stanley said as he tossed over a clean legal pad and a ballpoint to Sasha.

"He comes to office with good credentials, regarding public service, and education. And he did teach Constitutional law in Chicago." Karen added, as Mark winced.

"Let's return to the drug example for a moment," Mark said. "When I prescribe a drug for a patient, I have been given that assurance that it has been thoroughly evaluated as to potential side effects and even death."

"If we use that example with regard to Obama, he never met any of the required tests. The origin of his birth is still questioned by many. We have no school records to evaluate. The fact that he went to Harvard Law could be a plus, but the reason why nothing he ever wrote there, has been published, remains a mystery. So, I believe that negates it as a good."

"Not quite," Pastor Joe began. "I believe, as in a debate, we take what might be offered as assets and debits, and then come up with a decision as to which of the arguments has merit. At any rate, I believe the onus is on our two students here."

"How about the fact that he wants to do good. He wants everyone to have health care. He wants everyone to have a job. He has made many promises to do just that." Jillian said.

"But," Sasha interjected, "all political candidates make promises, with the best example being Hope and Change to influence and or fool the electorate to vote for him or her."

"Since you are both correct," Father Anthony said, "the purpose of the exercise, like my example of a drug disclaimer, is to see if the candidate met the qualifications, was transparent with regard to personal history and did no harm. "

"Based upon that," Stanley said. "Should his brand, or candidacy ever have been put out on the political market?"

Rabbi Tom rubbed his shoulders. "The wood fire and the topic have given me a great thirst." He said.

"I made a big pitcher of lemonade. Hold on a sec." Jennie said as she went into the kitchen. Karen offered to help and followed. Jillian wrote down as much as she remembered, while they waited for the women.

When Jennie and Karen returned with the lemonade and glasses, the group settled down and continued.

Father Anthony, noting that everyone was waiting for him, pursued his thoughts. "Perhaps we should now dwell on how the healthcare law and religion, particularly Catholicism are at odds. First from a purely Constitutional consideration, no one should be compelled to buy or buy into a product, whether it is health insurance or for that matter a mode of transportation. The former, however, interferes with an individual's religious principles when it comes to abortion, contraception or birth control, by virtue of drugs such as the 'morning after pill'."

"That is my own and the belief of millions of Catholics. However, we have no right to force our belief on those who think otherwise. For that matter, nor does the government or its leaders. It is what I consider the obnoxious, egotistical point of view of the administration and the people they employ, that they know better than anyone else, irks me." Father Anthony added.

"What about the argument that with regard to a corporation that the right of its owner who might be a Catholic, and wishes not to offer health insurance that provides any of that which you mentioned, is trumped by governmental rules and regulations?" Rabbi Tom asked.

"Glad you used the word trumped, since the attempt to interfere with the moral and religious right of an American who provides jobs to his people is a trumped up argument. The office of the attorney general is as partisan as it can be." Father Anthony replied. "Look at Fast and Furious."

Sasha was about to add her two cents to his last portion, but Stanley stood and stretched his legs. "Got to get used to nine holes of golf in this weather. Aches the bones." He turned to Pastor Joe. "Any thoughts on religion in the context we are examining?"

Pastor Joe stood as well. "While we, and I mean my flock, does not necessarily espouse all of the objections to obamacare voiced by others, I agree with Father Anthony as to governments attempt to usurp common principles. Where then is the separation of Church and State our liberal friends offer as argument?"

"Perhaps Mark can shed some light, as a physicians as to why he believes that the health care law will destroy the quality of care all of us, even the 30 million or 40 million or now the 50 million people whom Obama tells us daily, are without health care. Those numbers change so often, they are as reliable as the weekly unemployment figures."

Stanley turned to Karen. "You are involved with patients and their needs, feel free to speak as well. Mark what would you like to bring up?" Stanley resumed his seat.

"I am tired of hearing the argument that Republicans have offered no alternative to obamacare. That is an absolute lie. To date on six different occasions, Republicans sent bills to the Senate offering health care reform, but not an overwhelming destructive law that puts one sixth of our economy at risk, and would not have caused 5 million plus, people to lose their health care. However Reid et al refused to bring the bills even for debate. And if he did and were passed, Obama would veto them. So much for Obama's lies about working with Republicans." Mark said.

Stanley snickered. "If he ever worked with them it would remove his ability to blame them. Well he would still have George W. Bush to blame, and he would have the race card to play."

"I agree," Mark said. "Even though we enjoy the best healthcare, some of the best doctors and hospitals in the world, there is definitely room for improvement." Karen nodded in agreement. "I concur with the House proposals, that we need tort reform to lower liability costs for doctors. People should be able to cross state lines to get insurance to make for more competition. Small business should be able to pool their efforts for more reasonable premiums."

"I have no issue with pre-existing condition modifications, but they might have a larger deductible. As far as kids being on their folks policy until age 26, that is just liberal bull shit, only meant to gather in the young vote. And if you think about it, that was a huge miscalculation by HHS." Mark added.

"We still need to insure more people," Karen said.

"If Obama did not screw up our economy with his idiotic policies, there would be less unemployment. More jobs. More money, so people could afford to spend more. As it is obamacare has caused employers to let people go, and reduce work hours for many, just to stay afloat. No one is turned away from a hospital or denied care, and anyone who says so is lying." Stanley's face was flushed.

"Calm down, Stanley. I really do not want to test obamacare right now with you in the hospital." Jennie said.

"We are losing good doctors every day. Fewer young people are applying to medical schools. Soon we will be like Canada and England with the death rate from cancer going through the roof." Stanley would not be deterred. Mark went over and tried to calm him down.

"This Dad is an exercise for the girls, and certainly they get the point we all are making." Mark said.

They continued to keep the discussion centered on obamacare. At one point, Stanley noticed that Fox was about to show all of the times Obama made statements about keeping your insurance and doctors, accentuated each time with a verbal period, and turned up the sound. When he suggested that this more than utterings misspoken, Karen showed her liberal side by complaining that nothing the president ever said or did would be accepted.

"Let's get over the assumption that conservatives find fault because he is black." Mark said. "He has lied about everything so many times, there is no way of knowing if he has ever told the truth about anything."

Rabbi Tom spoke up. "Unfortunately, Mark is correct. I voted for Obama in 2008 because I really believed he might make a difference."

He collected his thoughts. "Well, unfortunately, he did. He has proceeded to destroy our economy, and our standing in the world. Just look at what he has done to Israel. As much as I would like to turn the other cheek, I find it impossible. Needless too say he did not get my vote in the last election."

Jennie's suggestion that they break for tea and freshly baked scones, received complete approval. Stanley, after checking his watch suggested that they work through tea, because he hoped for a dinner without politics and he still had to do some last minute marinade for the ribs. He assured the latter came from a cow, but added that there was always chicken.

"Okay, Mark said. "Healthcare.gov or whatever it's called was opened up with no preliminary testing, and no provision, even if was up and running, and glitch free, that the software could connect personal information with the insurance companies. That code is yet to be written. Obama was in such a hurry to shoot this crap out, he never asked if it would work. At any rate that is what has been alleged. People are losing their health care in droves. In California, where they are bragging about their successes, the majority of people really signed up, what ever that means, are Medicaid. This means they put no cash into the system, so Obama will further drain Medicare, since young people will not sign up, and Obama needs their cash. Even if the suggestion that premiums might be lowered, and they will not be lowered, deductibles will go through the roof."

Sasha raised her hand then pulled it back. "I heard yesterday that someplace in Florida, there are only seven pediatricians for over 207 thousand children. Could that happen here as well?"

"Of course, Stanley said. "In forcing doctors out of provider insurance groups, and with doctors taking early retirement, there will be an enormous shortage."

"And that is what the president really wants?" Karen asked suspiciously,

"That is exactly what he wants. He wants a one-payer system. He will say anything and do anything to achieve that result. That you can take to the bank." Stanley said.

"So you really believe that young people will not buy into obamacare? Karen said. "Is there anything that the administration can do to change their minds?"

Sasha laughed. "I am certain Obama would even get Hollywood involved to promote it. Well from my point of view as a young person who might eventually be adversely affected, and an avid fan of the ghoul movies, I would think that if Jay Carney, could make us all believe Obama was a vampire, some of the more stupid and unformed might think buying in was a good thing."

Stanley applauded as Karen frowned. Jillian looked at Karen and wondered if she was the right person for her brother.

Pastor Joe leaned forward. "Sasha and Jillian. You two have enough yet?"

Jillian sat up from her prone position and rubbed the fingers of her right hand. "My fingers hurt from writing, Pastor Joe, but, hey, this is my assignment, Sasha's and the rest of the class. We have a lot of stuff to cover.

"How about you Karen?" Mark inquired.

Karen stretched out her slim 5ft 6" frame on the floor and moved her arms and legs as she was making a snow angel. "I'm fine." She said.

"In that case, I would like follow up on something Anthony, here began earlier." Pastor Joe said.

"Please", Jillian said.

"I am very disturbed by what appears to be the government's push to separate religion not only from State, but from its people. Happy Holiday? Happy Holiday. It is Merry Christmas. Who does that really offend? Taking carols out of the schools. Taking the pledge of allegiance out, since it mentions God to placate people who believe in nothing, and attempting to justify it by claiming not enough time in the school day. Obama celebrates our Easter with his version of an Easter egg roll with spoons and wooden eggs." Pastor Joe said.

"I am not comfortable judging someone else's beliefs. But in the case of the atheists, if they are happy believing in nothing, who am I to object. Let them live and be well." Rabbi Tom said. "But, and this is a big but. Why do they feel the need to butt into the business of people who take pleasure in a Christmas tree, or a crèche, or singing carols or exchanging gifts, or searching for real colored eggs. Is that politically correct? Who cares?"

"Well said, Joe and Tom." Father Anthony said, as he looked to Stanley to redirect the discussion.

"Any suggestions, Jillian or Sasha?" Stanley asked.

"Yes," Sasha said. "I would like to focus on Benghazi and the rest of the scandals."

"You have the floor Sasha. You really have the floor." Stanley laughed at his joke. "And you are referring to those 'phoney scandals'."

"Where was the president when our consulate was attacked? Why was not help sent, and why for five days did he and Rice blame it on a video?" Sasha asked.

"May I take a stab at this?" Mark asked. "It happened in September of 2012, two months before the presidential election. Exposing him for what he really is would have hurt him politically. I believe that sums it up."

"But Hillary was Secretary of State and the embassies and consulates were her domain. She also, even when they met the families as the bodies were returned to Dover AFB, maintained that the video was the one and only cause." Karen sat upright. "Oh my God, she covered it up with the rest, and I was thinking of voting for her if she ran."

"Mark laughed. "By George, I think she's got it!"

"Moving on," Jillian said, checking the list of issues she had made.

"Hold on," Stanley said. "Before we do move on, Mark, would you like to summarize our thoughts on obamacare?

"I believe I can deal with that." Mark said. "We have a law passed by a Democratic House, a Democratic Senate and signed by a Democratic president, without one Republican vote, and read by no one prior to voting in its favor. As the unions and large corporations and even members of his party put pressure on the president, he caved and changed the law unilaterally to grant certain waivers or extensions. It became immediately clear that small business would suffer, so employees were cut and hours reduced to get around the law. More unemployment, and less wages were now the alternative to paying a fine far less costly than obeying the law. The promises made on a continuum and echoed by party hacks that everyone could keep their insurance, their doctors and their hospitals has been showed to be a lie used for the purpose of re-election. The website rushed for unknown reasons has been a failure and is still incomplete. Obama suddenly changes the law again regarding the reinstatement of millions of Americans who have suddenly had their health insurance dropped by their insurance companies, because they did not meet ACA standards. His ability to suddenly make these changes is being questioned."

"All of his changes are being looked at regarding whether it is constitutional. Insurance companies just to reduce their costs, have dropped many doctors. It is reasonable to assume that the cost of prescription drugs, both generic and non-generic will skyrocket. Deductibles will be unreachable driving many sick people and their families to the poverty level. There is also a board of bureaucrats, who will make life and death decisions based upon cost effectiveness and moneys available." Mark added.

"Let me interrupt, for a moment, Mark." Pastor Joe said. "To what purpose?"

"Simply put," Mark responded. "By making health insurance unaffordable, by making deductibles unreasonable, by increasing the cost of prescriptions, by taxing medical devices, by forcing Americans to purchase a product they don't want, by allowing twenty-six year olds to stay on the family policy, by reducing services, by stealing money from Medicare, and by pressing more people into Medicaid, Obama will ultimately have what he really wants, and that is a one payer system, national health or socialized medicine. The next aside we will hear will be that insurance companies will be allowed to renege on accepting people with pre-existing conditions. This all will lead to the destruction of the best health care system in the world. Oh and I forgot to mention that Healthcare.gov does not protect your personal and economic information from hackers, or so-called navigators, none of whom are required to undergo background checks."

Karen put her hands to her forehead. "Oh, my, God. As a social worker I work to get the best for my clients. I, like so many, got suckered into all of this by believing the lies they told. Mark, you were and are right. I was wrong. I am so sorry."

Jennie stood up. "I think that this might be a good time to break for some liquid refreshment, while Karen and the girls help me prepare some dinner. I am hungry. We can continue afterwards."

"If I might make an observation," Pastor Joe interjected. "Billions of taxpayer's dollars have been wasted on a merit less program, designed to fail."

TEN

Scandals

Stanley, Mark, Pastor Joe and Father Anthony watched the end of a college football game, drinking Manhattans. Rabbi Tom was called away to visit a member of the congregation who had suddenly taken ill, and had been admitted to the hospital in Kingston. He said he would return if he could, but not to wait dinner on his account.

After a dinner of ribs, chicken and sides of garlic mashed potatoes, they were too full to even think about the dessert of banana bread topped with pear preserves, Stanley had canned the previous year.

Father Anthony patted his stomach. "After that feast, I am not certain I can think about anything political, but I will try."

They all settled back into their original places on the floor and sofas, with the exception of the rabbi who had not returned.

"I can envision two more hours to skim the surface of the scandals, since we only know they exist, but as to why they occurred, there has been no explanation or acceptance of responsibility from any one in government, including Mr. Obama, who has repeatedly used the Sgt. Schultz defense." Stanley said.

Jillian, Sasha, Karen and Mark looked to Stanley for an explanation.

"Sorry, forgot some of us are older and still remember television when it was both clean and funny. There was a program, that now would be called a sitcom, about American and British prisoners in a Nazi prison camp during WWII." Stanley laughed.

"It was called 'Hogan's Heroes', and one of the characters was a jolly German guard, whose response to any questions was 'I know nothing'. This has become the motto for Obama and members of his administration. We have heard this in response to Fast and Furious, Benghazi, NSA, IRS, and of course obamacare." Stanley concluded his explanation.

Jillian could not at all relate to what her father referenced, but did not tell him. "Okay, can someone summarize each of the scandals, so we can deal with them later." She said.

"Wait." Stanley said. "Tomorrow is Sunday, we have plenty of time."

"Mr. Ashton," Sasha said. "My head is almost filled to bursting. All good stuff, mind you, but I had better get home first thing in the morning. And I just bet Karen and Mark have better things to do. You did say that you wanted to explore Woodstock, right, Karen?"

Karen smiled at her newly found friend. "Actually I did say that."

"Okay, we clean up the scandals tonight, and tomorrow everyone is on their own. Karen and I do have to get back to the Bronx late in the afternoon." Mark advised.

"Oh stay for Sunday dinner," Jennie pleaded. "It is an easy drive down to the Bronx, and we hardly ever see you."

"Don't let your heart be troubled, to quote Sean Hannity, I think Karen and I might be seeing more of you, as long as our schedules permit." Mark said, as he sat down on the floor next to Karen.

After the table had been cleared and all of the dishes secured in the dishwasher, the group without Rabbi Tom, reconvened in the living room.

"So," Sasha said. "I would like to tackle a few issues still within the realm of obamacare. Father Anthony and Pastor Joe, are you required to purchase health insurance?"

Father Anthony decided to go first. "I have only myself who might need health care insurance, and I am fortunate that the diocese does provided it." Joe, what is your experience?"

"Well," Joe said with a wry smile. "Ministers do not make much, and even with a family, we have fewer needs. On average, Anthony, we earn perhaps in the range of $35,000 per year, so we are grateful when our church elders make certain we have health insurance."

Sasha smiled. "All right. So, do you both have to have a policy that included birth control, contraception, and maternity care? Certainly an over kill for you Father Anthony."

"That is an issue, we have been fighting between the government and the Catholic Church," Anthony said. "I believe it was initially brought to the forefront by that Georgetown Law school person, who felt that everyone should pay for her sexual excesses. And do not forget abortion, which is not supposed to be covered."

"To each his own, or her own," Pastor Joe said. "I did give a sermon on the matter and got a hundred percent positive response in my favor. Do I wish the parish to include this or the other matters?" Not at all. Another day, another lie."

"Time to really move on to the scandals. However, the information is scant since no one has come forth to admit wrong doing." Stanley said. "Let's start with Benghazi.

Jillian turned to a blank page on her legal pad and prepared to take more notes.

"What this government, I believe, allowed to happen in Benghazi, and the obfuscation of the cause and events, will be as big as smear on the so-called Obama legacy than any of the other scandals we know of or have yet to be uncovered. Look up obfuscation. It is a good word." Stanley paused momentarily. Now on September 11, 2012, four brave Americans, including our Ambassador to Libya, his adjutant and two other American heroes were brutally murdered, and the Ambassador body desecrated. This we know is fact by virtue of eyewitnesses brave enough to come forward, despite the government's alleged warning against doing so. Our government did not protect them and no attempt was made to save them from their horrible fate.   Susan Rice, the U.N. Ambassador, paraded herself before television cameras, proclaiming that it was caused by a 'spontaneous' uprising created by a video. No one, even Hillary Clinton, then Secretary of State or Obama, has ever come forth to really apologize or retract the lie."

"Why would they lie like that?" Jillian asked.

"Because it happened barely two months before the presidential election and Obama thought it would impair his chances. That was not the only election quieting lie, since it has been alleged that the Unemployment figures were also fudged to make Americans believe that things were getting better." Stanley replied.

"Do you want to speak about when the four bodies were returned to Dover Air Force Base?" Sasha asked.

"I was about to do just that, Sasha. In attendance, as I recall were Hillary Clinton, Joe Biden and Obama. I am not certain if Rice was there. Anyway, all of them assured the grieving families that what had happened was undeniably due to the video, and that he, Obama would find who was responsible and have them pay for their crimes." He thought for a moment and sighed.

"To date, nothing that anyone is aware of, has been done, and the families are still demanding justice. This demand continues to fall upon deaf ears. The House of Representatives, at least the Republican side, is still trying to break through the denials to get some answer." Stanley said. "That is all we have been allowed to know. We have never been told where Obama was that terrible September night. September 11. You would think someone might have been on the alert."

"Okay," Jillian said. "Fast and Furious." Father Anthony and Pastor Joe asked to be excused, since they had to revise their sermons for the next morning at church.

"I plan to interject morality in government, with being, of course as specific regarding who and what. I think my flock has enough intelligence to comprehend my intent." Father Anthony said.

"As will I." Pastor Joe said. "I know I speak for Father Anthony in thanking you all for your hospitality and a very enlightening afternoon and evening." He looked at Sasha and Jillian. "You girls have a tough assignment, but I know you will work hard on your essay." He had wanted to include that they do the right thing, but decided not to.

After the two clerics left, Mark asked Karen if she had become weary. She replied that she would stay up as long as everyone else did.

Stanley started a discourse of the failed gunrunner scandal. "Unfortunately, we do not have all the facts on this either. There was some effort by the previous administration to pull a sting exercise on Mexican cartel gunrunners. What we do know is that an American border patrol agent was killed with one of the weapons someone smuggled into Mexico. The problem is the lies and continued obfuscations; there's that word again, that we have to deal with. To date the families, again, have been provided with little or no information."

"Anything else on that Daddy?" Jillian asked.

"That's about it. Another lie. There was an issue with a Fox reporter named James Rosen, but I don't have a lot of information other than his first and fourth amendment rights may have been violated. Briefly, I think it is important to touch on Solyndra."

"Never heard of that." Jillian said.

"Goodness your teacher did not talk about that in class." What a surprise." Stanley said with sarcasm. "There is a man by the name of Al Gore, who was once our Vice President, second only to Hillary and William Jefferson Clinton, and so angered by losing to George W. Bush in 2000, with, he became an advocate of Global Warming, while allegedly making millions if not billions of dollars. Global Warming has been rejected by the most intelligent minds, while promoted by the few who envisioned so many lobby dollars stuffed in so many white envelopes. Just as an aside, if one would even accept the outrageous poring of carbon dioxide into the stratosphere, we must question why promoters such as Gore, maintain energy consuming estates and fuel consuming jets that easily send enormous amounts of that gas that humans normally exhale up, up and away. With that in mind, a solar panel manufacturer, whose ass-kissing of Obama led to their being given millions, if not billions, failed miserably. I forget to mention that the higher echelon of Solyndra had contributed, allegedly, into the Obama rush for election and re-election. We also have an array of windmills of questionable value that have been killing the eagle, our national bird, but I do not recall any tree hugging anti-pipe line conservationists yelling foul."

"Stanley, I hope you took your blood pressure meds this morning." Jennie said.

"That I did do. That I did do." He said, and added. "Before obamacare makes the cost of all medication unreachable in fairness to all that is. We must begin on Benghazi, since it has the potential for removing the next viable teflon, democratic candidate. H. Clinton."

"Hold for a moment while I write what you said about Global Warming." Sasha said as she turned to the next clean sheet on her legal pad. "Is that the same as Cap and Trade?"

"Cap and Trade is an illegal solution to a non existing Global Warming issue, but Obama is trying to finesse that using forced EPA regulations." Stanley answered. "Obama is bypassing Congress in every way he can by ordering his flunky sub cabinet appointees to make rules at the whim of the White House and our shadow government. Have you noticed that Valerie Jarrette is present in every meeting of import? Her claim to fame has got to be something she has on both the president and his wife. She knew them well during the old Chicago days. And by the way, she was born in Iran."

"Daddy, we must get on with Benghazi." Jillian said. "And I am getting weary."

"Okay, suppose, we finish with Benghazi tonight and mention NSA and IRS tomorrow morning, and that should do it. The rest will be up to you." Stanley said as he looked at Sasha and Jillian.

"This is what we have been allowed to know." Stanley began. "Any one wishing to contribute should feel free to do so. After the Libyan revolution and the elimination of Khadafi, Libya remained a dangerous place. There had been attacks on British facilities in Benghazi, shortly before the murders of the Ambassador and three other Americans on September 11." Stanley shrugged.

"It has been reported from testimony at Congressional hearings that Ambassador Stevens asked for increased security. However, no one, including the then Secretary of State, Hillary Clinton responded." Stanley continued.

Stanley asked Jennie to bring him some lemonade. "We do not know why Ambassador Stevens was in an insecure area such as the Benghazi consulate, protected (sic) by locals. It has been suggested by some that there may have been some evidence of gun running to the Syrian rebels, but that has never been substantiated. Well prepared, and well-armed terrorists attacked both the consulate and then went on to attack the annex on that terrible night. They set fire to the consulate, killed and mutilated Ambassador Stevens, prior to attacking what was believed to be a safe house a mile away. This all took place in about seven hours, yet our president was apparently oblivious, along with Clinton, and no help was forthcoming. Then came one of many lies. The 'incident' was blamed on a video, and this lie was perpetuated by the Ambassador to the U.N. Susan Rice on five television stations. It was never suggested by anyone in the Obama administration that this was not a lie. The president came out with his usual bombastic statement that the perpetrators would not go unpunished. We all know how that worked out. The poor jerk that made the video, I believe is still in a California jail. I have already discussed the disgrace fostered upon the brave American's families when the bodies were brought to Dover, AFB."

Both girls had tears in their eyes. No one had any questions to ask.

Jillian sighed. "I believe I have more than enough information now, to write my essay. I just have to organize all of my thoughts."

"I agree," Sasha offered. "I for one am exhausted. Would it be okay if I stayed over again?"

"Absolutely, Jennie said. Why don't you call your folks and let them know."

The adults stayed up for another hour, after the girls went to bed.

ELEVEN

More Scandals

The smell of freshly brewed coffee and fried bacon brought Jillian and Sasha down to the kitchen where they found Karen, Mark and the Ashtons deep in conversation.

"Good morning young ladies," Stanley said. "Ready for eggs and bacon? And you have the choice of tea, coffee or hot chocolate." Both of the girls opted for hot chocolate laced with small marshmallows. Sasha thought that Karen had an unusual glow about her, and immediately ascribed it to a better understanding with Mark.

"You two have responded beyond expectations with your ability to concentrate and absorb so much information in such a short time." Stanley said. "So, I propose that we spend no more than two hours and that, should," he said, as he glanced at his watch, "Bring us to near noon."

Mark smiled. "And the Giants play Green Bay at one. Let's have an in the house tail-gater feast. Karen and I will have to leave after the game."

After breakfast, the six went back into the living room and settled into the spaces they had occupied during the long afternoon and evening of the previous day.

"Any questions regarding what we have discussed so far?" Stanley asked.

"I have a question," Karen said. "Regarding what has been suggested as scandals, is it at all possible that President Obama just did not know?"

Mark's face darkened. "The office of the Presidency has certain responsibilities, none of which the occupant can conveniently escape for any reason. Harry Truman, a democrat, clearly stated that the 'buck stops with him'. If Obama was unaware of all of these issues, he should have been, and gets no pass from me. The lies are yet another issue, unbecoming of the office, and apparently used to retain possession of that office."

Stanley frowned momentarily. Then his demeanor brightened. "The NSA has negated the fourth amendment for millions of Americans, and allegedly for people of the world not privy to rules as laid out in our Constitution. It is called spying in the name of National Security and is now up for severe scrutiny."

"That Snowden fellow blew that open. The coverage on him has been fairly constant." Sasha said.

"Needless to say, it is another blot on the presidency." Stanley advised. "A Fox reporter and his family were allegedly investigated by our Justice Department, perhaps infringing upon their fourth amendment rights. Unjustified exploration of their phones and emails. The IRS is being investigated by Congressional committees for unfairly treating people and corporations, whose opinions and politics were adverse to those of the current administration. This is among many issues still being stonewalled by the president. So much for that great promise that this administration was to be the most transparent ever. Just another packet of lies and the lies keep coming. There is so much that we could expand upon. Unless you girls need more, I could go for a long walk on the golf course. How about you Mark?"

Mark looked at Karen. "I think I am already getting vibes that she has become a golf widow. I did promise to shop with her in town, before the game."

"We never discussed the game, but if we can go to town first, I will help with cooking the tailgate or whatever." Karen said.

Both girls laughed at the last remark. "I am cool. How about you Sasha?"

Sasha said she felt she had enough information. "I really appreciate everything," she said. "I don't want to overstay my welcome and not be invited back." Mark offered to drive her home before they went into Woodstock. Sasha really had hoped to be invited to tag along, but that invitation never materialized.

Later, when Mark and Karen returned with gifts purchased at a local boutique, Jennie protested. "This was absolutely not necessary." Jennie said.

"I know," Mark replied, "but I have a very persistent girl friend here." Karen blushed.

Stanley looked at the time displayed on the cable box, and announced that the game was about to begin. "Hope your Green Bay lovin cousin, Justin, will not be too disappointed when they lose badly to our New York Giants."

"They don't even play in New York," Jillian protested, "and haven't for years."

"Well, they do belong to us New Yawkers, and not those Joizy people," Stanley said with a laugh.

He went into the kitchen, and returned after a while with a tray of beers and a bowl of buttered popcorn. Glancing at the screen and noting that the required number of commercials had to be aired before the kickoff, he pulled a handful of popcorn from the bowl and began to munch while he spoke.

"I may have already said this, but since I find obamacare so repulsive with each passing day of liberal, democratic denials, I shall repeat. Does anyone recall seeing a television program called Amos and Andy?" Mark and Karen said they had not, and Jennie observed that she must have been a baby.

Stanley shrugged his shoulders and glared lovingly at his wife. "Well my Dad told me that two white gentlemen, named Freeman and Gosden, originated Amos and Andy on radio in the 1940s. It was a friendly spoof of the black community in Harlem. Later the program was brought to television with black actors, and the characters of Amos and Andy, Lightning, Madam Queen and the Kingfish moved seamlessly into the new media. It was meant to be funny and not mean spirited, although it angered some of the more politically correct enough to have it removed, never to be seen again."

Jillian got up to grab some popcorn. "And your point, Daddy is what?" She asked.

"My point is, that one of the characters, the Kingfish, who never held a job, and never ran a legitimate business always had these hair brain schemes that got everyone into trouble, that Amos had to fix. In Barach Hussain Obama, we have our Kingfish! Obamacare, his foreign policy, or lack thereof, and his constant bumbling have made this country, the laughing stock of the world. Coin toss. Game on!"

During half time with the Giants ahead 17 to 10, Jillian reviewed some of her notes, only to be interrupted by the ring tone on her cell phone, that she had assigned to Sasha.

"We forgot that damn outline!" Sasha said with disgust.

"You are right!" Jillian answered. "Let me pass it by Daddy and Mark, and I'll call you back."

"Outlines are an excellent way to organize your thoughts." Mark suggested. "If you need some help, we are here."

"I, for one am not convinced. It is my suspicious nature as a lawyer." Stanley remarked. "What's the issue?"

"Well, Ms. Jones wants it on her desk at school tomorrow morning." Jillian said. "One of the guys said it could be spying."

"That guy," Stanley said. "Is very astute. You have your assignment. The outline is for you and not for her. She will see your positions when she reads your essays."

"She's their teacher." Karen interjected. "Perhaps, she just wants to keep them on track."

"Doubt that." Stanley said, pressing the mute button. "She wants to make certain, that you are writing what she wants you to write, to please her own political preference, or that of some other interested party. Look at how the assignment is worded, and you will quickly get my meaning."

Jillian reviewed the assignment, and all agreed that Stanley was probably correct.

"Okay," Mark said. "Make a neutral outline, listing things that Obama preens about, like creating jobs, killing bin Laden, the best of obamacare which would be the issue of pre-existing conditions. Add stuff like his Nobel peace prize. The objective is to be non-committal." He looked at his sister. I never asked what you planned to write in your final draft."

"So much is riding on this. Certainly, my future. This is going to be a tough decision. I had better call Sasha back." Jillian said, as she ran up to her room.

TWELVE

The Outline

It was Monday morning, and as Jillian, Sasha and most of the class waited out side a locked gymnasium, they shared the progress they had made. Her voice down to a whisper, Jillian offered suggestions made by her brother regarding the structure of the outline. The Dean's secretary then came by and informed them that the gym instructor had been called away on family matters, and they were to spend the next forty-five minutes at the library.

In the stacks, far away from the front desk and the prying eyes of the librarian, Ms. Penelope G. Clinton, Jillian, Sasha, and five of their classmates sat on the floor discussing how to deal with Ms. Jones. Jillian showed them the outline she had constructed on her legal pad.

"How much of the class will be willing to tell the truth?" Sasha asked.

"I am not certain yet if it is worth the agony of my telling the truth about, Him." Jillian whispered. "Right now, I plan to bide my time, write my essay and turn it in on time. She never said we had to follow our outlines to the letter. I am so confused."

"Jillian, look at it this way." Sasha said. "It really doesn't matter if there is a consensus in the class one way or the other. It all boils down to an individual decision, and what ever happens happens."

"I am concerned that certain people will think ill of me." Kelly observed.

"Certainly not your father." Sasha said.

"Oh, not Dad, but certainly most of the members of our church." Kelly said.

"People will just have to get over this black and white thing." Sasha said. "My opinion is that he is a bad president, who happens to be black. People made a mistake. They will have to be honest and just suck it up!"

A loud shush came from somewhere toward the front of the library. "I would not be surprised if they had the books wired." Sasha said, getting up. "Bell's going to ring in a minute. Time to move on."

They entered the classroom and were surprised to find Ms. Jones already at her desk. The teacher rose from her chair and motioned for the class to take their seats. Ms. Jones knew that no one was late, but checked her watch and scowled nevertheless. On the blackboard, written in large letters were the words. 'PLACE THE OUTLINES ON MY DESK.'

After counting twenty-five pieces left by members of the class, she looked up. "Three of you people are absent due to, well, supposed illness, so that leaves, let me see Jillian and Sasha. I would like your outlines now, and they will be considered in how your essay is graded."

Sasha's hand immediately shot up. "I have my outline, but it was my understanding that we were to debate the pros and cons in the assignment, as one would do in any debate."

"Do not smart mouth me young lady. You all were given a copy of the assignment, so that needs no further explanation." Ms. Jones shot back. "Jillian Ashton. Your outline please, and yours as well, Sasha."

She took the papers handed to her by Sasha and Jillian and placed them with the others. After asking the class to remove the school provided iPads from their backpacks, she provided a website for them to review, that dealt with issues of gays and lesbians in the military. This she advised would give them the opportunity to understand the "ills these folks were subject to", and give her time to review the outlines.

Using the rare opportunity to use their iPads in the classroom, most of the class quickly became disinterested in the assignment, and played games or emailed each other with the sound off. Jillian and Sasha, however, did check a number of websites, but quickly understanding their biased nature, they moved on to E-books.

After a half-hour, the teacher took all of the outlines from the desk and placed them in alphabetical order. Then she removed a paper from a manila folder. It contained information, culled from the front office, which detailed each family's personal preferences on a number of topics. This had been collected and added to the bland but required responses each child and parent had responded to, when acceptance to the school was to be determined. The former had been instituted in the winter of 2010, when the school found it necessary to apply for government subsidies.

After making some notations on a pad, she looked up over her reading glasses and frowned. "People. It would seem that there are many similarities in your outlines. Any explanation?" She asked.

Again, Sasha's hand flew up along with Jillian, Kelly and five other members of the class. Ms. Jones called upon Kelly. "But the assignment was so restrictive in nature, it would stand to reason that the outlines would show some similarity." Kelly said.

"I see." Ms. Jones responded acerbically. "I would expect more of you for many reasons." She looked down at a paper on her desk and removed her reading glasses. The corners of her eyes revealed as little mirth as suggested by the down-turned corners of her mouth. "I can understand better now. How much of your assignment was provided by your father?"

"I will not deny that I share my school work with my parents," Kelly tried to control her anger. "But, no. I play fair. I also do my own work. Therefore what ever grade I get, must reflect upon me and not my parents for any reason!"

"You been taken sass lessons from Sasha, here? Girl. I will put up with none of that." Members of the class smirked at her fall back to the street talk.

The rest of the class provided reasonable responses as to the similarities of their outlines, but also advised they had not seen anything their classmates had written. Sasha, biting her tongue, provided a neutral but similar answer that Ms. Jones had no recourse, but to reluctantly accept. But, still not letting go, she decided to read Jillian's outline to the class.

She quickly reviewed the short list that represented Jillian's outline. Then she re-read the paper and scratched her head with a pencil. She went over the document once more assuming she might have left out something, and looked at Jillian.

"Miss Ashton. You reside in Woodstock. That is correct?" Jillian nodded. "Is your family registered to vote there? She asked.

"Excuse me, Ms. Jones. But I cannot see where that is anyone's business. If you have some issues with my outline, tell me and I shall make whatever corrections needed." Jillian responded as politely as possible.

Ms. Jones made some notations on the paper. "Here, come get your outline and see that you stick to it. And that goes for the rest of you folks." At that moment, the period bell rang and the class was dismissed.

"Doesn't it just piss you all off when they refer to us as folks or people. There are times, some of these assholes never know our names." Sasha said, loud enough for almost everyone to hear. Fortunately, the door to their last class remained closed.

Her friends snickered, but most of them had heard her utter more directed profanities. Nancy put her finger to her lips and then suggested they move on to the next class. Jillian asked that they meet at lunch, and at table outside, far away from faculty, since the temperature at noon was to hit a balmy high of 57'.

They cleaned off a wooden table and benches that sat just outside the door leading back into the cafeteria. The monitor in charge asked them just to bring all refuse inside after they were finished. Then Jillian, Kelly, Sasha, Jay Takamushi, Nancy and Carmen Petti ate their unauthorized lunches.

"I would like you to share your outline with us, Jillian." Sasha said. "She has already reviewed them, and wrote whatever on her secret paper. Does anyone know what that is anyway?"

"Just to play safe, I typed my real outline onto my iPad." Jillian said as she opened it up.

Kelly folded up the wax paper that had housed her illegal ham and swiss sandwich, and wiped her mouth with a napkin. "When I brought up my outline as the bell rang, Ms. Jones had gone to the blackboard, so I took a quick look. What I could gather was that it was a list with our names, where we lived and some voting information. There was a lot more but I did not wish to be caught. I am on her shit list already." She said.

Jennie opened the door just as Jillian reached for the doorknob. "You are unusually early, "She said.

"Bus was almost empty since lot of kids had rides, so there were fewer stops." Jillian responded. "Any snacks? I am hungry."

"Made some banana bread. It's in the fridge." Jennie said. "I have to run down to the market for some veggies. Anything special you want me to pick up?" Jennie asked.

"How about a bunch of carrots? I saw just a few poor souls left and they really looked dried up and scraggly." Jillian called out to her mother. She watched momentarily, as Jennie backed her Kia out onto the road and closed the door.

She had just walked into the kitchen when the house phone rang. Jillian was surprised to hear Ms. Jones' voice at the other end.

"Jillian. This is Ms. Jones. Did I reach you at a bad time?" The teacher asked.

"Your are calling me at home is quite unusual. Is something wrong?" Jillian was not sure what to say.

"I wanted to speak with you about your outline." Her voice was softer and more congenial than usual. "There were a few things I found questionable, actually disturbing. I recall you making some remark that President Obama's likeness should be added to Mt. Rushmore a while back. Actually this is what prompted my choice of assignment for the essay. I am correct that was your suggestion? Yes?"

Jillian was not certain where this conversation was going. "Yes. Ms. Jones. I recall saying something like that."

"And I recall your telling me that when you discussed this with your folks, your Father was not terribly pleased. Am I correct?" The teacher asked.

"Something like that." Jillian repeated herself. "Why are you calling me?" Jillian was becoming nervous.

"Have you changed your mind?" The teacher appeared more assertive.

"Why these questions Ms. Jones?" Jillian asked impatiently.

"In your outline, you have listed for discussion such items as Benghazi, the IRS and NSA and something you refer to as gun running to Mexico, in addition to the affordable care act which really should be the cornerstone of your essay." The teacher's voice again had softened.

Jillian attempted to defuse the moment and stall for time. "I listed a number of topics, including the killing of bin laden. Not all of them do I plan to use, and an outline is only an outline. Things could be added and things deleted." She offered.

"Yes, I understand, Jillian." The teacher responded. "I hope you will be very careful as to your final assessment. The school administration would like to have all of my students of like mind, if you know what I mean."

"Actually I do not." Jillian responded. "Do you plan to call the entire class this way?"

"No. Not every one in the class. Just those I believe to be sitting on the fence. This essay is as important to us as to you all. After all, colleges will be looking at the grades you get this semester, as well as those you will accrue in your senior year."

"Should I consider this to be a threat of some kind?" Jillian asked.

"Of course not, my Dear. Perhaps you should just think of my call as a teaching moment. You do plan to be in school tomorrow?" Ms. Jones inquired.

"Absolutely." Jillian responded.

"Excellent. We shall talk more then, Jillian." The line went dead.

Stanley Ashton seemed agitated when he arrived home.

"Tough decisions at the hospital?" Jennie asked. "We waited dinner for you. Some pasta and fresh veggies I will have warm up for us. And I made you a Manhattan cocktail. Would you call Jillian and have her set the table?" Jennie went back into the kitchen.

Stanley took a sip from his cocktail and savored its taste. "Jillian! You busy doing homework?" He called up the stairs that led to his daughter's room.

Jillian came down and gave Stanley a hug and a kiss. "I'll be right back. I forgot to set the dinner table." She said.

Jennie brought a large dish loaded with bow tie pasta and fresh vegetables, that she had cooked in garlic and olive oil. Each sprinkled an ample amount of dried Parmesan cheese on their dinners. "Got a call from Karen today. She wanted to thank us again for the weekend. I really like her."

"Who knows?" Stanley said as he chewed a fork full of pasta. "She might be the right one for Mark."

"You guys have any feeling about their sleeping together over the weekend?" Jillian asked.

"I just have the feeling it was not the first time." Stanley said. "But do not interpret that as a general relaxation of rules of the house, young lady."

"Oh, I don't even have a boyfriend." Jillian said coyly.

Stanley scooped up the last of the pasta on his plate and wiped his mouth with a napkin. "Good choice." He finished the last of his Manhattan, and pushed his chair back from the table.

"Jillian, did you get a call from your History teacher this evening?" Stanley asked.

"Yes, I was about to tell you, but how do you know about that?" Jillian asked.

"As I was about to get into my car at the hospital parking lot, Malcolm Storey came over to me. He was actually enraged." Stanley said.

"What happened to cause that?" Jennie asked.

"He said that the Jones woman called Kelly earlier this evening, and made what Malcolm considered threatening comments." Stanley looked at his daughter.

"Ms. Jones called just as you left for the market, Mom. I was so surprised." Jillian said.

"See if you can go over the conversation word for word as you best recall." Stanley advised as Jennie got up to clear the dishes. "No, Stay Jen. You should hear this as well. The dishes can wait."

Jillian went over what she believed to be word for word, since she also wrote down the conversation, immediately after it concluded.

"Too bad you didn't record it." Stanley observed.

"I was too nervous to even think about that. But if she called every student, we will have a lot of damning information. Won't we, Daddy? Jillian asked.

"That will depend upon what she said to each of them." Stanley responded. Jennie cleared the dishes and returned with slices of banana bread slathered with pear butter.

"So what else did Malcolm say?" Jennie asked.

"He is roaring mad, and plans to go to the school first thing in the morning and confront the Dean, and then the teacher. I told him that I did not think it was a good idea." Stanley said. "I just believe it best to collect as much negative stuff about them quietly. There will probably be a firestorm if even half of the kids produce inflammatory essays. Then I would suggest calling a town hall meeting at the school, and give those who wish, a forum in which to vent their anger."

"You really believe it might come to this, Stanley?" Jennie asked.

"It is time that we parents retake an interest in what our children are being taught in both the private and public schools. We have to see the curricula before the start of the year and make certain it is followed as closely as Ms. Jones wants your outlines followed. Personally, I have had enough of liberal brainwashing to which the children are subjected, and now beginning at an earlier age."

"My cell is ringing up in my room, and its Kelly's ring tone." Jillian said.

"Would you mind bringing it down with you? If Kelly does not mind I would like to hear what she has to say." Stanley said.

Jillian returned with her phone. "I have it on speaker. Kell said it was okay."

"Kelly, this Jillian's Dad. Is your father at home?"

"No, Mr. Ashton, he was called back to the hospital for an emergency, and Mom is spending a few hours stocking the shelves at the food pantry." Kelly responded.

Stanley asked Kelly to relate her conversation. "

"I tell you the truth. I don't know if I remember everything, but what I do remember is what I believed to be a threat, and I lost my cool." Kelly said.

"And she responded how?" Stanley asked.

"She denied emphatically it was a threat and called it a teaching moment." Kelly responded.

"Same with me." Jillian jumped in.

"Kelly, you didn't happen to record the conversation did you?" Stanley inquired.

"No, Mr. Ashton. I was in too much of a panic to even think of it." She replied.

"I bet that's true of all of the students she called." Jennie said.

"But," Stanley said. "She doesn't know that to be a fact. If need be, we might just put that doubt in her mind later."

"What should we do? My Dad is so furious." Kelly said.

"I think I diffused some of his anger, but he still plans to have a conversation with the Dean tomorrow. I did convince him not to confront Ms. Jones yet. Keeping her in the dark could improve our position later." Stanley said.

"What do you mean, later, Mr. Ashton?" Kelly asked, her voice quivering.

"Suffice it to say. You all go to school tomorrow, business as usual. Make no waves. Do not discuss your essays with anyone now. Even your classmates. Except those whom you absolutely trust. Like Sasha for example. In fact, see if you can tie her into a conference call now." Stanley said.

Jennie was amazed with the ease that Jillian setup the conference call between the three phones. Sasha was apprised of what had transpired.

"No," she said. "I received no call and I have been home since my brother dropped me off at the house. If you want to know what I think, is that she has written me off and just assumes a flunking grade for me on the essay. I refuse to back down and will just have to deal with it. Actually, I had nothing really inflammatory in my outline. I also did not have anything complimentary." Sasha laughed nervously.

"I believe that the real arm twisting is yet to come when they find that more of the school finds the president to be a liar, and his policies detrimental. There has to be a lot of money involved. I should ask for an audit of the schools books." Stanley said.

"Can you really do that?" Jessie said.

"Unfortunately, no," Stanley admitted, "but it will certainly make them uncomfortable, and then, again, someone on the Board might get nervous enough to push for an audit. I also just have a feeling that more than just the curriculum has to be scoped. I want to have the matter in which potential teaching candidates are vetted evaluated, and who makes the decisions regarding what texts are purchased."

"You still have our legal backs?" Sasha asked.

"That, my darling, you can absolutely count on." Stanley responded.

THIRTEEN

Confrontation Aborted

Malcolm Storey arrived at the school at 7:30 a.m. and went directly to the front office. Much to his chagrin, he was told by an unfriendly secretary, that the Dean was not expected for an hour, and also had appointments scheduled all morning.

"He will see me!" Malcolm said as he took a seat and picked up a copy of the New York Times. Once an avid disciple of the weekend puzzle, he had not purchased the Times for over ten years, disgusted with their liberal policies, and what he considered front-page editorials, offered as news.

"Suit yourself, Mr. Storey." The woman who identified herself as Alana Colmes said, as she walked into an adjoining room, returning with a hot cup of coffee that she placed on her desk.

"I believe that twelve years of grade school, eight years of college and medical school and six years of residency, not to mention being licensed to practice medicine in three states has earned me the title of Doctor. And thank you, no I do not wish to have a cup of coffee." Malcolm said as he tossed aside every part of the paper except the Sports page.

"I apologize. I didn't know." The secretary stammered.

He just stared at her without telling her what he really thought. His first appointment was not until 11:30 and he had already made hospital rounds having spent the night there with a sick patient.

An hour went by, and the Dean had not arrived. "Your boss keeps a rather loose schedule, and I have yet to see his appointments show up." Alana Colmes' face reddened. "It would seem to me that what ever salary that our tuitions pay for, are well wasted on him." Malcolm said.

"I have no control over that." Colmes said.

"But you do have control over the truth!" He retorted. She was about to make some kind of reply but he waved her off when his cell phone rang. Without another word he left the office.

The I.D indicated that it was Stanley Ashton. "Malcolm," Stanley said. " Fill me in."

Malcolm explained what had or actually had not transpired, and how pissed off he was getting.

"Just as well," Stanley said. "There will undoubtedly be a confrontation and it is long coming. However, we should hold back all of our ammunition, and I use that term figuratively since I do not own a weapon. Where are you now?"

"Just getting into my car. I'll go back to the office. I want to write down some things I was thinking about." Malcolm said.

"Like give me a for instance." Stanley said.

"Well, briefly. It will be about what I call the new slavery. The slavery of entitlements." Malcolm responded. "School buses are coming in so I had better leave before I get boxed in."

Kelly looked out of the bus window and saw her father leave the parking lot. "Oh, my" She said. "I hope he didn't create a stir."

Ms. Jones was not in the room when the class had assembled and the final bell had rung. A few moments later, Christina Matthews entered, and informed them that Ms. Jones had taken a personal day, and they would be on their own to work on their essays, or read ahead in their texts, and that someone would check on them periodically. Sasha and Jillian had her in a sophomore English class and thought her to be mean spirited, pompous and contemptibly liberal. Well at least Sasha thought up the last part. It was clear to both that she did not follow the White House diet.

"Look, we are on our own, assuming that the room is not wired." Sasha said. Taz Patel was assigned to monitor the door. "This is a good time since we are all together, to speak our minds. How many of you got a phone call from her yesterday? Let's see a show of hands." Everyone raised their hands, of course, except Sasha.

Each in term told of their phone conversation, and no one was quick enough to think of recording the conversation. When questioned as to how many in the class were worried about the effect the essay might have on their acceptance to a college of their choice, all hands raised. When she asked how many would write an essay based upon principle, half the class raised their hands. It was clear that many more wanted to but might choose not to do so.

"I, for one, plan to write exactly how I feel, sort of if I was give the Con side of a debate, but I plan to look at the Pro side as well, so in effect I will take both sides, and come up with a conclusion. What do you all think?" Sasha asked.

Everyone said they believed it to be a fair approach, but they agreed that the assignment was set up in a way to assure a certain conclusion. They all offered that their parents were pissed off, even the ones who leaned precariously to the left.

"Well, what's the plan?" Kelly asked. "I saw my father leaving as the bus drove into the parking lot. I hope he did not say anything we will regret. I thought he was still at the hospital making rounds."

"My Dad said he would try to get a hold of him this morning." Jillian said. "We conduct business as usual. Keep a low profile. Do our class work and no confrontation since, what ever we each decide about the assignment, we really decide separately. So keep a cool head and turn your essays in on time next week. This is not a matter of mob rule. For instance like what is happening in our United States Senate. Ooops, sorry. No one will be condemned for what they write. At least not by us."

FOURTEEN

Cabal

Dean Roland Hannah's secretary, Alana Colmes knew very well that he would not be in until noon, thus her story of scheduled appointments was a fabrication. However, her job and healthcare provided, depended upon her ability to protect her employer at all cost. She was not a fool, but rather a well-educated individual, who had lost a lucrative job when her company downsized in anticipation of the business destructive high cost of bowing to the new health care law requirements. Realizing the direction the school was taking politically, she switched to a party that would be more accepted by the administration and many members of its Board of Trustees, thus meeting the requirement for employment. She had been taken aback by the sudden appearance of the well-dressed man whose name she knew, but never met, and now aware that he was what was appropriately addressed as African-American. Aware that he felt insulted by the manner in which she had treated him, she nevertheless believed she had done exactly what was expected of her.

The waiter had just poured coffee, when Davida Jones took her seat, joining the four others at the busy Red Hook diner. Despite the early hour, the restaurant was exceptionally busy at this time of the morning as it would be for the rest of the day. Seated well back near the restrooms, one could have a conversation that would guarantee ultimate privacy.

Roland Hannah was at best described as overweight, bald, and not particularly attractive. His sloe eyes that slanted down toward the bridge of his nose, and surrounded by darkened circles, gave evidence of sleepless nights. There was just something about his demeanor that turned every one off. Yet, some how he had become a leading educator, and Dean of a prestigious, pricey private school.

Certainly the fact that he had a lesbian sister who could have passed for his twin, did not necessarily lend itself to acceptance in this quasi-conservative community. However, even though she had ample exposure in her role as a news contributor on Fox, few in this upstate New York town made the connection. Nevertheless, he had the credentials and demeanor that gave the majority of the Board to reason to hire him.

Hannah greeted Davida Jones after a brief reprimand as to her tardiness, and asked her to sit. The one member of the Board present was the attorney, Murray Gannif. Both Edgar Fluecke and Vernon Jarretts were members of the faculty, and well known to her. Fluecke was a graduate of George Washington, and Jarretts had majored in Middle Eastern affairs, and had some vague association with a law school in Chicago. It had never been clearly defined, exactly what his contribution was to the school or its students. It did not matter since Hannah vouched for his ability and value, and would never entertain any discussions that might have the appearance of being derogatory.

The Dean ordered eggs and pancakes for the table with a number of sides of bacon, sausage and ham. As the food was delivered, the four dove into it, as if it might be their last meal. The cost was of no concern since the Dean had a carte blanche credit card that appeared to be limitless, and overlooked by Murray Gannif, who continued to stuff himself to the gills.

Their waitress cleared the table of their empty plates and asked if they wished anything else. Dean Hannah observed the next table being served an ample supply of French toast laced with fresh blueberries, but thought better of it.

"Perhaps a pot of coffee," he said, knowing that it would give them time to address the reason for their being there.

"Anyone have a pressing need to be somewhere else?" Hannah asked.

Jones said she had taken a personal day, while Fluecke and Jarretts both explained they had late afternoon classes. Ganiff had no restraints, he offered, except those imposed upon him by his wife who currently was skiing in the French Alps.

"Excellent," Hannah said. "Ms. Jones, or if I may Davida, do we have a problem regarding your classes and their class work?" He waited for a response. "Are you holding something back Davida?"

"There is a problem that I am certain I shall be able to resolve." She replied.

"We must not have anything but that which is absolute." Hannah said. "Have I missed our mark in any way, Gannif?"

The Board attorney took a sip of coffee. "It is no secret that we are running somewhat low on funding. It is also no secret that we will, the school that is, benefit from government grants," Ganniff responded, somewhat reluctant to offer sensitive information to non-Board members.

"And government grants or funding be that as it may, requires certain absolutes. Am I correct?" Hannah asked.

Ganiff smiled. "To be sure, and it also requires, unfortunately, the palm oiling of certain local and Albany based politicos as well. Without them there is no assurance that Washington will provide the monies to keep the school afloat. There is the never-ending one hand washing the other. Even the money we might receive in grants, some of which will find its way back into the pockets of local politicians."

"And on and on it goes." Jones said.

"Excellent," Jarretts remarked. "I do believe you've got it. And this makes keeping your class in line regarding its glorification of our president that much more significant."

"Unfortunately there are outliers." Jones said.

"How many might that be Davida?" Hannah asked.

"Not certain." She responded.

"You had better the bloody hell be, and make the corrections to assure 100%." Hannah said angrily.

"That, I am afraid will not be possible." Davida Jones answered.

"Anything is possible if the threat is realistic." Ganiff offered.

"My students are not stupid. I went as far to call almost all of them last evening." She responded.

"Did you threaten them in any way?" Jarretts asked.

"Not in so many words." Davida responded.

"And could any of those words have been recorded?" Hannah asked.

"I was careful, but I never thought of that." Jones stammered.

"How many students will not comply?" Ganiff asked.

"I only know of two. Kelly Storey and Sasha Finkel, from Saugerties. I do believe the others are more fearful."

Hannah took a sip of coffee and made a face. It was cold. "The Jew and the Black girl. You cannot control at least one of your kind?"

"Sasha's family is very conservative. Her father is a pediatrician. Kelly Storey's father is a physician, as well, and unfortunately understands obamacare. Two of sixty, considering the size of the two classes should not negate the grant. Should it?" Davida Jones asked.

"The Ashton girl. Her father is an attorney. You neglected to mention her." Hannah said.

"Jillian? I at one time thought her to be a believer in the liberal cause." She paused. "Right now. I do not know from our conversation last evening. She is non-committal, but could be a ring leader to swing her class either way."

"It would be expedient and to your benefit to have her swing in the more appropriate direction. Threaten her if you must." Ganiff said.

"Not in so many words, I may have already." Davida Jones said as she stood. "I have some things I must attend to. Please excuse me. The breakfast was exceptional."

After she left, Hannah turned to Ganiff. "How many members of the Board can we depend upon for support?"

"Not as many as we would wish. There are those with children in the school, after all." Ganiff responded.

Hannah shook his head. "That may unfortunately prove to be a problem. We do have some who might wish to expand their influence while seeking re-election. Let's use them as a battering ram if need be or might the word pawn be better?"

FIFTEEN

Intimidation

Stanley returned home after nine, the hospital's Board of Trustees meeting having crawled through an agenda that included both short and long range planning issues that would have to be postponed because of obamacare. The crux of the matter was that neither could be intelligently or fiscally dealt with because of all of the restrictions, regulations and selected waivers that appeared daily, some canceling out those that had surfaced the previous day. It was clear to most of the members of the Board, that the hospital and for that matter most hospitals might be forced to close. One wag brought up Nancy Pelosi's quote "if you pass the bill, you will find out what is in it." The language that followed could not be placed in the minutes. Although, the Hospital did no R and D, it would feel the severe hit from the medical device tax, along with every other hospital and manufacturer of braces, and replacement parts already on the market or still in the research phase.

Jennie met him with a shaker whose amber contents she poured into a chilled cocktail glass. "This was a dinner meeting?" She asked.

Stanley gave her a kiss and took a sip from the glass. "Needed that, Jen. Yes we had dinner. The usual chicken something. I have always maintained that the Hospital either bought out Perdue or the dietician is somehow related to its owners." He laughed. "Just kidding. Meeting was tedious for the obvious reason. We don't know if there will be a hospital next year. There was a time when insurance companies and HMOs reduced their hospital reimbursements drastically, and when hospitals would not agree to the cut, we lost most of the patients in their system, and some doctors as well."

He took a sip. "Now, with obamacare, we may, as a hospital, be forced to remove doctors, insurers or choose not to participate. The bastards in Washington will figure out a way to remove Medicare and Medicaid as a punishment. Not that reimbursements for either are substantial."

"Thornton Dick called around six." Jennie said. "He said it was urgent for him to speak with you, but he was on his way over to Albany for some late legislative meeting. I will never understand how he ever got elected."

"Nothing to understand. He is a liberal democrat, who like too many of them, are obsessed with power. Did he give any clue as to what he wanted?" Stanley asked.

"Not at all. But his daughter Nancy is in some of Jillian's classes, you know." Jennie offered.

"Jillian home?" Stanley asked.

"Upstairs with Sasha, doing homework." Jennie responded.

Stanley walked to the stairs that led to the upper bedrooms, and called to his daughter. "Hope you two are working independently on that essay." He called out, as the phone rang. The caller I.D on the television screen indicated it was Dick.

"Stanley, Thornton Dick here. Hope I haven't got you at a bad time."

"Not at all, Thornton, I actually was just about to ring you back. What's up? Stanley asked.

"I would like to have a face to face talk with you man to man." Thornton said.

"About what?" Stanley asked.

"About this thing the our kids have gotten themselves into." Dick responded.

"Are they in some sort of trouble? If, so, it's news to me." Stanley said.

"Look, you are aware of the essay assignment, given to the History class. Why are you involving yourself in the kid's schoolwork?" Dick said testily.

"Jillian is writing her essay on her own. So what might you be accusing me of?" Stanley asked.

"You know that you are trying to sway the kids to your way of thinking." Dick replied.

"I am just acting like a parent and not a politician. Seems to me that you cannot make the same claim." Stanley responded. "Just who has gotten to you about whatever it is that has placed a bug up your ass?"

"No such thing." Dick's voice softened. "I thought it would be good for us to meet and hash this out."

"Tell you what. If what is concerning you apparently has something to do with the students in that class, I would think it appropriate to meet with as many of their parents willing and able to do so." Stanley responded.

"We don't need the whole class involved, do we?" Dick asked.

"I think we would, unless you are accusing me of doing something underhanded." Stanley retorted, his patience waning.

"Er, not at all!" Dick stammered. "Exactly what is your role in all of this?"

"My role? I am Jillian Ashton's father. Jillian is a junior in school and a free spirit, whose judgment I will trust in whatever way she chooses with regard to the essay assignment. Therefore I have her back." Stanley said.

"As an attorney, I presume." Dick retorted. "And in regard to the rest of the class?"

"I defend people who believe they have been wronged. End of story. Make what you wish of it. Anything else you need to discuss?" Stanley inquired.

"No. That about does it." Thornton Dick said, as he hung up the phone.

Stanley waited a few seconds and then dialed back the number. It was busy as he expected.

"Who were you calling, Stan?" Jennie asked, as Sasha and Jillian bounded down the stairs.

"I was calling Thornton back, but I knew his line would be busy. I would guess he was calling to report to whoever put him up to this. And if I had to make an educated guess, I would say it was Dean Hannah." Stanley said.

"Was that Nancy Dick's father?" Sasha asked.

"Yes, it was. He was fishing for information, almost accusing me of starting an insurrection regarding your assignment." Stanley said.

"Oh, I don't want this to cause you any trouble." Jillian said.

"Stick to you guns Jillian, and just do what ever you believe to be the right thing." Stanley said.

"I hate to ask but I need a ride home," Sasha said. "My brother was supposed to pick me up, but something came up. I could call a cab."

"Don't think about a cab," Jennie said. "Get your coats, and Jillian and I will get you back to Saugerties."

"I guess that your Dad's not home, Sasha. I did want to speak with him. Tell you what. He could call any time before 11:30 tonight and that would be fine." Stanley said. Sasha's father did call at around ten p.m. Stanley explained that Thornton Dick had called, and apparently was pressured to do so. He outlined the plan of action that might have to be taken if the girls' teacher used her own political preferences in grade determination. But he suggested to allow the kids to deal with their essays on an individual basis, and hoped that every parent would be proactive with regard to explaining what was really happening in the country.

When Stanley arrived at his office at the hospital the next morning, he found a message that a Mr. Thornton Dick had called and he wished to be called back. It was the same cell number Stanley had called back the previous evening and found to be busy.

"Thornton Dick here." He looked at the caller I.D. "Stanley, thank you for calling me back so promptly." There was a definite change in his tone. "About your suggestion to meet with all of the parents. I am fine with that. I believe I can accommodate them at my home."

"Actually, I did run it by Sasha Finkel's father, and he has a rather large room in his home that can accommodate at least fifty people if needed." Stanley responded with a smile. He had already discussed a venue with Finkel, and both agreed that meeting at Dick's home might prove troublesome. Who knows how many unnoticed ears might be sitting in on their conversations."

"You really think that there would be that many parents interested enough to require an area that large. I do have ample room." Dick responded nervously.

"We are good to go. I shall certainly let you know when." Stanley said. "You will have to excuse me, now Thornton, I have some urgent hospital business to attend to." He observed the call waiting blinking, and pressed a button on the console. It was Jennie.

"I hope I did not interrupt anything," Jennie said. I just wanted to see if you might like to have lunch."

"I would love to." Stanley said. "No you did not interrupt and thing. That was Thornton. And you know. He really is a Dick!"

SIXTEEN

Intrigue

Immediately after his conversation with Stanley Ashton had concluded, Thornton Dick dialed the main number at the Academy.

"Dean Hannah, please. This is Assemblyman Thornton Dick." He frequently used his political advantage to get him into places.

The phone rang three times and Hannah picked up. "Yes, Thornton, have you learned any more since our conversation last evening?"

"As a matter a fact, yes. There may be a problem." Dick responded.

"What sort of problem? I thought I told you to agree to a meeting at your home." Hannah said impatiently.

"There is to be a meeting, not at my home, but at David Finkel's in Saugerties. Ashton said that it would accommodate more people." Dick answered.

"More people. Just how many of them are in on this. We can twist a few arms, but, how many more?" Hannah asked.

"That I am not certain." Dick responded.

"Hmmm. Perhaps you could suggest the need for a member of the school administration to be present, to answer any questions that might come up. And that would be me, naturally." Hannah said.

"I will try Dean Hannah, but I doubt if Ashton will agree to it." Dick responded.

"Then cold call some of the others and suggest it." Hannah demanded.

"Actually, the only one I know is Dave Finkel, and for some reason I doubt if that will be acceptable." Dick said.

"Why would that be?" Hannah asked. "Are they doing something illegal?"

"With Ashton presiding, I suspect it will be to the letter of the law." Dick said.

"Well, then, just pick someone and make the call." Hannah said. "You know. Try Malcolm what's his name, Storey. Yes. Storey. He and Davida Jones have something in common." Hannah said. Had he been in the office the preceding morning, Malcolm Storey would be the last person he would have suggested.

Just before Stanley was about to leave for lunch, his secretary buzzed his intercom. "Could you have a few minutes for Dr. Storey. He is here in the outer office," Lisa DiStefano asked.

"Of course." He responded. Malcolm Storey entered, and Stanley signaled for him to take a seat, as he picked up his cell phone and dialed. "Hi, Jen. Order me a Cobb salad and an ice tea. I will be there shortly. Love you too."

"If this is not a good time." Dr. Storey said.

"Not at all Mal. You would not be here just to shoot the breeze. Actually I had meant to call you anyway." Ashton said.

"You will never guess who I got a call from this morning. Right in the middle of student rounds, and he would not be deterred." Malcolm said.

"Let me guess. Our Assemblyman Thornton B. Dick." Stanley said.

"I never knew Thornton had a middle name. What does the B stand for?" Malcolm asked.

"Never mind. What did he want?" Stanley asked.

"Apparently something about a parent meeting for which he wanted me to subscribe to Dean Hannah's attendance." Malcolm laughed. "Little did he know what I really feel about our not so illustrious Dean."

"Believe me you were not left out of the loop. This all materialized last night. The parents are meeting to, how shall I put it, to get a better understanding of a current assignment in the History Class, in addition to a bit of enlightenment, regarding what our kids are really being taught here and elsewhere in this country under the guise of education."

"Go on. What ever it is. You know you will have my support. We have had this conversation so many times, but now it apparently has grown legs." Malcolm said.

"Why do you suppose, Dick really called you?" Stanley asked.

"Now, Stanley, why do you suppose?"

"Right. Anyhow, Dick called me last night to arrange a one on one with me, which I believe was orchestrated by the person who wants to intrude. I refused and suggested that any parent willing to attend should, and that was immediately put down." Stanley smiled.

"When I sort of suggested that I did not need his permission, he backed off and obviously called the master puppeteer. Reminds me of the way Washington does business."

"No matter. Count me in, and I shall get coverage if need be." Storey said

"The meeting will be at David Finkel's. He guaranteed enough space. The date and time we still have to work out, but it would best be this week." Stanley said. He checked his watch. "I will call you later, Malcolm. Got to meet Jennie for lunch."

The server brought their lunch order just as Stanley arrived at a small local place called Mezzaluna, where they had always found the food to be excellent as well as the service. During bites of tomato and tuna, Stanley brought Jennie up to speed.

"I still don't understand why Dick picked Malcolm to call. He is more conservative than you. If that is possible." Jennie remarked.

"Lunch is superb, to quote one of our more liberal acquaintances. Perhaps I should leave that to your imagination." Stanley said, as he gulped some ice tea to offset the sting of an errant chili pepper that had found its way into his salad bowl.

The ring on Stanley's cell phone gave Jennie cause to frown. "I do have a law practice to attend to," he remarked. "It's David Finkel. Yes David. That will work for us. See you then. Wait suppose we split the list alphabetically. There should be ground rules. Yes. I will deal with that, but best to just suggest that it be a concerned parent meeting. I do have some other news but Jennie is grimacing over her pasta vera. Will call you later this afternoon. Tomorrow night at seven. I'll work out who you should call, if you will." Stanley said and hit the call end button.

"Now eat slowly and digest your food, and give me the cell phone." Jennie said.

"Yes Mommy," Stanley said with a broad smile.

To Jillian and the others, Current History seemed rather boring with Ms. Jones making no demands on the class, even allowing use of their iPads. Of course only for what ever was pertinent to the assignment, and the progressive movement of the early 1900's. Two biographies were assigned for the next school holiday. Theodore Roosevelt and Woodrow Wilson were two presidents with whom she felt the class should be familiar.

As the weather remained temperate, Jillian and her friends opted again to have their lunch outside, away from what they called the prying eyes of the food police. The group was all abuzz about the meetings that their parents were to attend, but neither Jillian nor Sasha chose to provide any information as to what might be discussed. In truth Stanley Ashton and David Finkel thought it best that the girls not be privy to the agenda still being developed by Stanley. If Davida Jones had any inkling as to what was transpiring, she gave no evidence, but just before the class was to end, Dean Hannah did come by to whisper in her ear.

Jillian was surprised to see her father already home when she entered the front door.

"Hi Hon," He said. "Check with Mom as to dinner that she did prepare for you. I think it is pepperoni pizza, and call your brother. He apparently has decided to move into Karen's apartment, so I guess this is serious. He said to call his cell." Stanley said.

"And what's with you guys? Date night in the middle of the week?" Jillian asked. "What's up?"

"Tell you what. Call your brother. Do work on your essay. Oh, and there might be more books for you to look at for info in my study. I left them on my desk."

Jennie came out dressed in black slacks, a turtleneck purchased during their last ski trip to Vail and comfortable flats. "Did Dad give you the lowdown on dinner? Just have to warm it up in the microwave. Doggies have been fed and they were out, so we'll let them out again when we return. Keep the light and TV on in the living room, and don't answer the door. Back door is locked. We have our phones."

"Gee whiz!" Jillian exclaimed. I am not a baby and you have gone out before. Oh. Please be careful driving and watch the speed limit." She laughed as she skipped down to the kitchen. When she heard the front door close, she dialed her cell phone. "Hi Sasha, something is on. Very hush hush. Mom and Dad left for somewhere."

"I know Jillian," Sasha said. "The party is at our house."

Stanley parked his Subaru on the street behind a Dodge truck, went around to the passenger side, and opened the door for Jennie. The driveway was filled with an array of upscale vehicles. They walked to the back of the large Tudor as instructed, and came to a one-story studio attached to the rear of the house. Above the door was signage denoting "JELENA's SCHOOL OF DANCE".

Jennie smiled. "Sasha never told me her mother was a dance teacher."

When Stanley opened the door, they came upon a spacious room, paneled in glass, and encircled with waist high metal bars. "Perhaps I shall finally learn plie," Stanley whispered.

"Hush and behave yourself. This is probably serious stuff." Jennie whispered back.

Considering how close Sasha and Jillian had become, they really had only infrequent meetings with David Finkel, who greeted them at the door. He wore a blue cashmere sweater, black slacks and sock less loafers.

"Jelena has a recital tonight in Kingston, so she will not be joining us. A number of parents are in the den enjoying some non-alcoholic refreshments as you suggested, and I am not certain how many more to expect." David said.

"Has the honorable Thornton Dick arrived yet?" Stanley asked, as Jennie squeezed his hand.

"No. Let's see if I remember the names of people who are inside. There's a Carissa Van Wagoner, Selma Morton, Granton Shultz, Bob Logan, and Reice Morales. I think I have got that correct." David Finkel offered.

"Is Reice a man or a woman?" Stanley said.

"Very much a man and presumably spends lots of time at the gym." Finkel answered.

"Both parents of kids able to come?" Jennie asked.

"Some of them are single parents. Carissa Van Wagoner and Bob Logan are both recently divorced. That was shared immediately." Finkel said with a laugh.

"Oh my," Jennie said. "This meeting could serve a dual purpose."

"Thank you for the observation, Jennie." Stanley said playfully. "Perhaps we should now call you Jentyl."

David Finkel laughed heartedly at Stanley's joke, as six people joined them, each carrying a bottle of water. Oddly enough, over the two and a half years that Jillian had attended the Academy, Stanley and Jennie had met Bob and Selma twice, because Jillian had been involved in projects with Jane Logan and Faith Morton.

There was a knock on the door, and five more people entered, and introduced themselves. Thornton Dick, however was not among them.

Stanley introduced Jennie and himself. "We will wait a few minutes for Assemblyman Dick, but in the meantime, I'd like to suggest the following. Everyone will have the opportunity to speak his or her mind, but we must stay on topic. I am not certain how much any of you were told as why we are here this evening. I have great concerns in what our children are being taught in their school. I have even greater concern as to what children are being taught all over this country, in the lower grades, the grades in which our children find themselves and in so many of our colleges and universities." He looked at his watch. "Oh if you have something to offer, wait until the previous speaker has said his or her piece. Best not to offer your name. Your opinion will suffice. I shall monitor to the best of my ability."

Thornton Dick stood outside THE JELENA SCHOOL OF DANCE, a cell phone seemingly attached to his right ear. Despite the cool temperature, he was sweating.

"I understand. But you must understand, I do not know all of the parents of the class. Yes, I will do the best I can, but bringing in a recording device would be too obvious. I will take copious notes." Dick said to Dean Hannah and ended the call.

Thornton Dick opened the door and saw many people he did not know. Since he was the elected representative from the district in which many lived, most knew of him.

"Great!" Stanley exclaimed. "The Assemblyman Dick has arrived."

SEVENTEEN

Confrontation

Stanley proceeded to lay down the ground rules. All cell phones had to be turned off, but everyone had been given the Finkel house phone number to be left with their children in case of emergency. Dick mildly objected to the fact that the only one to take notes would be Stanley, and questioned as to why no introductions had been made. Stanley indicated that it was understood that everyone in attendance had a child or children attending the Academy and therefore a common objective.

Stanley opened up his iPad. "Okay, since our Assemblyman Thornton Dick was instrumental in calling this meeting, perhaps he should begin with his concerns."

"Well, actually," Dick stammered. "I just wanted to talk about an issue that should concern all of us, and that is the fiscal strength of the school that all of our children attend."

"Great start," Stanley said. "What are the fiscal concerns? Is the Academy in danger of going bankrupt?"

"You already asked me that during our phone conversation." Dick responded testily.

"Correct," Stanley retorted, "And you never answered the question. This would be a good time to do so, since many of our children are in their junior and senior years, and if the school was in danger of failing, it could be devastating with regard to college application."

"No! No!" Dick said. "It's not that bad."

"So what exactly is it that troubles you?" David Finkel asked.

"Perhaps someone else should have their turn." Dick said, droplets of perspiration forming on his forehead.

"We don't wish to pressure you to say something that you cannot. Do we?" Stanley threw his thought out to the group. "Some water perhaps?" He said offering Dick a bottle. "Is there something you know that you cannot share with us? Your daughter Nancy, after all will be applying to colleges soon."

Dick took a long drink of water and wiped his lips with his hand. "This is information that cannot go any further than this room." Dick said. "Dean Hannah has applied for a substantial grant for the Academy which indeed is having financial issues. The grant is from the government, and the Board had to indicate total support for all and I mean all government policies."

Bob Logan raised his hand. "When you say government, you do not mean Albany. Is that correct?"

"I mean Federal Government, Washington, the White House." Dick said.

"Is this tantamount to making us, meaning the school, an offer we can't refuse?" Reice Morales asked.

"Something like that." Dick responded.

Stanley stood. "Now we are really getting to why we are all here, and it boils down to an assignment given to a History class, whose inference has become, toe the mark or else. What do we, as parents really know about what are children are being taught? Stanley asked. "Has any one ever attended a PTA meeting?"

Everyone shrugged their shoulders including Jennie and Thornton Dick.

121

"Do we have a PTA?" Jennie asked.

Selma Morton rose, and said that she had been involved in cake bake sale to raise some money for cheerleader pompoms, but recalled no other meetings that involved parental cooperation.

"We, as parents, myself included," Stanley said, "have been terribly remiss. No, we have been stupidly uninvolved in the schools curricula. They have our children almost eight hours a day, five days a week, almost twenty-six weeks a year, and none of us know what the hell they are being taught. Do we really have a handle on the credentials of their teachers?"

"Who are the members of the Board of Trustees, and why is there a financial crisis?" David Finkel asked. "And why don't we know about it?"

"Because none of us asked." Stanley said. "In the two history classes taught by Davida Jones, there are almost sixty students. Understanding that this meeting was called on short notice, look at how many of us have turned out. How many of us are on the Board of Trustees, or actually can name those who are?"

Jennie spoke up for the first time. "We now know some of the why. I think it time to look into the how, and this entire issue has come up because of an assignment given to our kids by someone I believe to be terribly biased and who, unfortunately could have the future of our children in her hands."

"Right!" Stanley said. "Now lets talk to the point. The business of the school's finances, its Treasurer, the Dean and its teachers are another matter we will get to. Let us hone in on the liberal bias of at least once teacher, and the threat held over the heads of our children."

"Look, I am a democrat, and elected official to the New York State Assembly. You all know that. I am probably setting myself up for disaster, even being here, and telling you that Dean Hannah has been putting pressure on me, also threatening to withhold political contribution to my campaign." Thornton Dick admitted. "But I owe it to my daughter to do the right thing. I cannot write her essay, nor can I take away what I have told her as to how it could effect my political career and our family."

Stanley stood again. "Look I make no bones about my political affiliation. I was a democrat. However, I voted independently more often that not. In the 2008 democratic primary I bit the bullet and voted for Obama against Hillary Clinton, because I did not believe he had chance to win against any Republican. I was wrong. And it has been proven I believe, that fifty-percent of the American people were wrong and are now deeply regretting their vote. After that election, with full understanding of the politics of Woodstock, I, we, decided to register as Republicans. We had our concerns living in a community that seems so biased, but we have chosen our friends carefully and our politics have not changed our daily life." He laughed. "Except, that is when I get pissed off reading some of the letters to the editor in the Woodstock Times. But I see a ray of hope with clear changes of attitude on the part of many in the community."

Stanley looked at Thornton Dick. "I have a question that has been bothering me for a long time now, Thornton. Do you agree with everything this White House has done in the past five years? Do you agree with everything the Senate majority leader has said and done? Do you believe the House Minority leader should be recalled along with a number of others? Is there a need for a black caucus? Do you believe in obamacare? There, that's a good start."

David Finkel started to speak but Bob Logan beat him to it. "Look. Our purpose is not to attack the Assemblyman."

Thornton Dick smiled. "I can defend myself thank you. I have had to do that all of my political life, and have the scars to prove that growing up was not an easy task. I am a democrat. Yes. But I am not a fool. Vomiting up the party line is a given when you are accosted by reporters or acting as a talking head or speaking as political strategist, what ever that really means." He finished the rest of his water.

"Do I agree with everything the White House has done? No. Not everything. I am very liberal in my belief that everyone deserves a fair shake, not necessarily a share not earned. Undeniable lies, I find very troubling, but I want my party to stay in power. However, the party that I became an advocate for is not the Democratic Party that I joined a number of years ago. I am not a player in national politics, nor do I believe I every will be one. I do work hard for my constituents, but I fumbled the ball when I allowed people to purchase my integrity, and that is all that has been purchased. I will pay a price for that in the next election. I shudder when I hear the White House stance on Benghazi, and the gun running in Mexico. I was very much in favor of the principle set forth by the Affordable Care Act. I did not like the lies the president told. No I never read any of its thousands of pages, but neither did my party members who voted for it. I am not a Socialist."

"Harry Reid does what he feels best for Harry Reid and the party and the country, in that order. Personally I believe him to be a weasel. Pelosi, well, I cannot fathom how she got as far as she has. Clearly she must have something on everybody." He paused to take a drink of water from a new bottle handed to him. "I think that should sum it up, pretty well."

Stanley walked over and playfully punched Dick in the shoulder. "You know. I believe I could even learn to like you. If I made an attempt to do so." He picked up his iPad and checked his notes.

"Okay. We'd better get back on track. Some of these people have to get back to their families. For any of you still sitting on the fence, I suggest two books. The first is Jerome Corsi's 'Obamanation.' The second is Obama's own book, the first one called 'Dreams of My Father'. Take into consideration that he met his father only once. Oh, and see if you can find the movie '2016' on Netflix or DVD. The reason I am suggesting this is to better understand the dilemma, our children are going through that is, if they did their research. Their assignment, good or bad, is their assignment, and they will have to approach it as if it were a debate, with each of them taking both sides. We cannot write their essays. We might read them if they chose to let us see them. So what is their dilemma? You all are aware of it, but it deserves repeating. If they write what that teacher has assigned, assuming good punctuation and grammar, they will get a good grade. If they write what they believe, not what we may or may not believe, they could put themselves in a position to get a bad grade, that their teacher has heavily weighted for the semester final grade. The implications are obvious since the grades they get will be reviewed upon application to college." Stanley looked for questions.

David Finkel was the first to speak. "So, Stanley. Is there a plan?" Bob and Selma echoed this as well.

Stanley looked at Thornton Dick. "A lot may depend upon Thornton here, and what he feels he is obliged to tell Hannah and the rest of them."

"What would you have me say?" Dick asked. "My daughter has as much to lose as the rest of the students, and she is more of a rebel than a democrat. I would be most proud if she did what her conscience dictated."

"This is what I suggest," Stanley said. "Provide nothing of import that will get back to the school administration."

"I agree," Bob Logan offered. "I would say that, we met and expressed our concerns about the assignment, but that we all agreed not to meddle."

Reice raised his hand. "I agree as well, but would add that we also raised some issues concerning lack of parental input regarding the curriculum, but leave out anything you shared about school finances for example."

"Great!" Stanley said. "Better to have them in a state of complacency. Thornton, you think you can pull that off?"

"Hell! Don't forget I am a politician." Dick said.

As the group started to exit, Stanley took David aside. "Thank you for offering the use of your home. We may need it again. I was surprised that Malcolm Storey did not call or show up. I assume he was busy with a patient." David advised him that he forgot to tell Stanley that Malcolm did call and could not attend. And both Dick and Malcolm are on the school Board."

"The essays are due in a week now." Stanley advised. "Let's see what happens. In any event, there is great need for a School Town Council to allow all of the parents to express their concerns. What happens with the essays will probably provide more fuel for the fire storm yet to come."

When, just before midnight, Thornton Dick received a call from Dean Hannah, whom he told very little of what had transpired, as he said he would.

EIGHTEEN

Obamacare and the Stockholm Syndrome

For every action, there is a reaction. Such has been the case for obamacare, given the more official name of affordable care act, and with every passing day, seen as not all affordable and with the expectation of limited care. Most reliable news providers have given at least both sides of the story in a fair and balanced manner. Those who look only to the biased media, with which they are most comfortable, continue to hear only the lies that this extension of government propaganda is readily willing to disseminate.

Hospitals are becoming more concerned with the manner in which they will long term plan, since there is no guarantee that they will have the resources, to look forward to needed upgrades and improvement in the delivery of health care to the communities they serve. Physicians have no idea what insurance plans that will allow their participation. They have not yet been informed if there will be penalties for not participating in Medicaid or Medicare. The people continue to panic, not knowing if they will have health care in 2014, even if they believe they might have actually 'selected a plan'. Those who have 'selected a plan' have been counted by the government in order to provide a false set of numbers, since the majority have not yet paid a required first month's premium.

Patients do not know if they will be able to keep the physicians with whom they have had a long, trusting relationship. Many hospitals may close and people living in more rural areas will be hurt the most. The elderly who need consistency, and are uncomfortable with sudden change will suffer, as a result along with the rest of us.

The majority of those people allegedly signed up opted for Medicaid, at least in California, since the premiums charged for government approved plans were either to high, the deductibles unrealistic or the financial ceiling on earnings to qualify was raised. Since Medicaid enrollees provide no moneys, and young people have shown no inclination to enroll, rather taking the penalty, who will fund this massive, idiotic, poorly devised program?

Who else must be held responsible for this disaster imposed upon an unsuspecting and poorly informed American public? Certainly the AMA, and State and County Medical Societies, whose only objectives seem to have been collecting dues, contributing to illogical political action funds, and having end of year parties. This year there will be little to celebrate or in years to come. If any one might be held to task for what has happened to medicine, one must look to many of the doctors whose greed has increased the cost of medical care, the attorneys who supported frivolous law suits, the insurance companies that settled cases rather than fight them, and the law makers who were paid off by lobbyists to ignore the need for tort reform.

This certainly is of no concern to the White House, since the real end result they are looking for is a single payer system that has failed in every country in which it has been implemented. People living under those oppressive systems have learned to 'love it' just as a captive learns to love his captor. Thus obamacare and the Stockholm syndrome become one and the same.

NINETEEN

The Health Care Delivery Dilemma

Stanley came home after ten p.m., but found Jennie waiting up for him, sitting by the fire reading a novel about Barbados, written by an author she had not read before.

"Sorry I am late." He said. "What was for dinner? I am starved." He explained that the emergency Board meeting at the hospital ran long over agenda, since so many members had questions to ask about the health care law.

"I'll warm up the Mac and cheese while you pour yourself a drink." She left the book she was reading on the sofa. "You would really like this book since you liked Michener's novels. It is called 'A LONG BEAT TO WINDWARD' and is a fictional story about Barbados but based on historical facts."

Jennie returned with a steaming plate of food and placed it on the dining room table. Stanley, who had been leafing through the book, smiled and joined her. "Jillian just loves Mac and cheese." She said. "No drink?"

"Water would be fine. There is so much I have to think about with all that is going on at the hospital." He said as he put a forkful of food in his mouth. "This is just great." He added. "Jillian in bed?"

"Working diligently on the essay." Jennie answered. "So what's going on?" She said as she poured ice water into a glass.

"Well, you know that the hospital has had to follow certain rules and regulations even before obamacare with respect to Medicare reimbursements. Certainly quality is a given, and there are benchmarks we must follow." He said.

"You said the meeting ran over since Board members had a lot of questions. That in itself is an unusual occurrence that you have repeatedly complained about." Jennie said.

Stanley scraped the last of the macaroni and cheese from his plate, and moved his chair back from the table, as two of the Aussies sitting at his feet waited for scraps that did not fall.

"Absolutely correct. It was remarkable that the meetings had become more of a social and dinner gathering, so I in no way begrudge staying late. There was real interest shown in what is going on." Stanley said. "If you are deep into your book, we can talk about this another time."

"Not at all. The book will be here, and it is an easy read. Makes one want to go back to Barbados." Jennie said. "Did you all come to any conclusions? I have had concerns regarding the Brain Trauma unit."

"The hospital and doctors are seriously considering forming an ACO in order to further conform to obamacare requirements, if it really continues to become a working reality." Stanley said. "The concept is being considered and implemented in many states now, you know."

"You have mentioned the ACO before, but I'm not certain I understand what it is." Jennie said.

"We have had an assortment of alphabet soups in the past, as you know. For instance, the MSO, the PPO, the HMO and so forth and so on." Stanley said. This mnemonic ACO stands for Accountable Care Organization, which could be a good thing without being under the scourge of Obamacare."

"And its purpose is what?" Jennie asked.

"I am just getting there. Perhaps I should review the current issues of providing health care from the hospital's point of view first, and you will have a better understanding of at least its Medicare reimbursement." Stanley took a long drink of water.

He refilled his glass and continued. "There is no question that the cost of providing health care has increased over the years, the envelope being pushed by the development of new and efficient diagnostic tests and equipment, the overuse of the emergency room for issues better evaluated in a physician's office, indigents and illegals effectively taking advantage of a system that turns no one away, and over utilization for a number of reasons that would be considered unjustified."

Jennie was about to ask a question. "Hold it for a minute Jen, and let me continue with my train of thought." Stanley said. "Let me back track about twenty years when surgeons and orthopedists held sway as far as the best paid specialists. Certain insurers allowed them to set the price for procedures such as the new concept of arthroscopy, which was great since it was a minimally invasive procedure. They all took courses as required, met the standards and suddenly the procedures acquired a big price tag. Now, since the procedures required little or no hospitalization, the specialists made less money, hence the hike in the cost of the surgery. They were now completely in control and the insurance companies went right along, since the actual payout was probably less, as far as hospital payments were concerned. Add to that the sudden surge of malpractice suits, justified or not, that escalated the cost of medical practice. Add to that the number of premature babies born, the infirmities and deaths, and the lawyers had a field day. As a result, the doctors had little choice but to increase their charges just to be able to afford to put their key in the door."

"I am listening. I want to get some coffee I brewed." Jennie said.

When she returned with coffee and slices of freshly baked banana bread, he continued. "Then California, from where the ridiculous and sublime seem to originate, came the HMO concept. Instead of refusing to participate, the medical community ignored its potential disaster, and resigned itself to the destruction of their practices, as huge numbers of immigrant physicians in their attempt to be accepted, embraced the concept. The HMO's sent erroneous, I am being kind, information to patients informing them that their doctors were players inducing them to join. The doctors had no recourse but to follow suit lest they lose all of their patients. The BIG LIE worked then, and it certainly seems like the BIG LIE works now." He drank some coffee and took a bite of banana bread as Jillian came bounding down the stairs.

"I am so into this essay!" She said. "I have been so blindly stupid. Is there more cake?"

"Your father is explaining what is wrong with medicine, Darling. There is more cake in the fridge. Help yourself." Jennie said.

Stanley purposely waited for Jillian to rejoin them, smiled and continued. "Physicians who were more into patient care than computerization became victims of their own foolish inadequacies. They were forced to spend thousands of dollars on computers and software and finally had to hire people just to deal with the paperwork, the sending of claims via the Internet and to determine if payment received was correct if at all received, and then to appeal the low or non-existent reimbursements."

"You mean that doctors were not paid at all for claims?" Jillian asked.

"The insurance companies and HMOs depended upon the fact that doctor's personnel who dealt with claim issues, would become so frustrated with speaking to ignorant people, being hung up upon accidentally, and of course, spending hours trying to recoup monies, that much of the paper work was shredded in sheer desperation, unbeknownst to their employers. I have been told that the position taken by some insurance companies was to have their personnel work up to 5 pm, and trash any and all claims left on their desks for that day, believing that physician's offices would forget about them. Millions of dollars were not paid as a result. With regard to Medicaid, many doctors who accepted Medicaid became frustrated that they had to resubmit claims so many times that the postage cost more than the reimbursement, that they would see patients without payment, because they were good and devoted people."

"Jillian, I had asked Dad about the ACO," Jennie said.

"I was just about to get to that." Stanley said. "But there is more leading up to the need for physicians to organize just for the purpose of monitoring the manner in which they practiced medicine. As an aside, let me just add that physicians blindly paid dues to the AMA and various state and county medical, societies who ultimately became instrumental in destroying the practice of medicine, because politics became more important than the patient's relationship to his or her doctor."

"This will not raise your blood pressure, Stanley, I hope." Jennie said.

"Actually, Jen, it is better I vent. Keeping all of this in me is much worse. I was about to tell you about the next major issue affecting hospitals and the practice of medicine, and it ultimately deals with over utilization of services."

"You are certain you don't wish to take a break, Stanley?" Jennie said.

"Mom. Dad's on a roll, and I find it all fascinating." Jillian said.

"She's correct, Jen. I am better than fine. Actually, venting is so healthy." Stanley said. "Let's see. I was speaking about over utilization. In the 1990s, we had an influx of foreign physicians. Most of them were quite good and contributed so much in the way of innovative medicine. Now, for the most part, they were trained here in our major hospitals, and chose by virtue of green card or citizenship to settle in the United States. Unfortunately, they remained close to the hospitals where the trained, for example on the East or West Coast and few ventured where they were most needed into rural areas. They were family orientated and once they established homes and practices, family members, many of whom were physicians followed. It is interesting that each of the physician family members chose specialties of medicine that might complement their practices. Unfortunately, this led to where patient referrals were to family and not necessarily out of medical necessity. This became more evident when a patient was admitted to hospital and the number of doctors, many of whom were related to the admitting physician, were called in for consultation. This served to extend a patient's hospitalization and increased the number of tests and radiological procedures ordered. This is better known as nepotism and has been an accepted procedure carried out by members of our elected officials."

Jennie looked up. "The ACO?"

"Right, what better way to offset these extra costs but to monitor physicians aligned with a hospital and define those who are considered outliers. In other words, the bad guys join or perhaps go into some other venture, and that is more a reality than a suggestion." Stanley remarked.

"So the best way, even not under the auspices of obamacare would be a physician hospital alliance that might improve quality and patient satisfaction, decrease costs by controlling unnecessary tests, unneeded consultations, and certainly decreasing the length of hospital stay, while providing optimal care. But, and this is a big but, and that is the relationship between the physician and his patient is sacrosanct." Stanley asked if Jennie might pour him a glass of Merlot.

"Let us deal now with the ACO concept that I have alluded to." Stanley said, after taking a sip of the red wine. "The ACO makes hospitals and physicians jointly responsible for providing quality care and reasonably reducing costs. This can be accomplished in two ways with the organization electing to operate with or without risk. In the former, the group maintains itself with seed money. If expenses are greater than expected costs come from earnings and profit may be non-existent. In the latter, it operates by accepting established rates of reimbursement, and must create its own checks and balances to stay profitable."

"You know Stan, we are already bare bones at the Brain Trauma clinic what with reduction in personnel and supplies." Jennie said. "How will the hospitals still provide quality of care and continue to cut costs? And I cannot believe there will be a consensus among the doctors."

"First the ACO will need a minimum of 5000 people enrolled. They may go out of network however, but it serves the hospital and doctors better for them to stay within. We all know that, for years, the LOS or length of stay has been tragically long due to over utilization. For example, there are groups of doctors, most of them foreigners who came here for residency programs and remained. Once established, they tend to bring other members of the family over who are healthcare professionals of varying ability. Once a patient has been admitted, it is the uncontrolled number of consultants called in through nepotism that creates a snafu extending patient stays."

"And this leads to more tests which require more tests or more of the ancillary services provided." Jennie offered.

"Exactly, and none of that can be tolerated by the ACO. There are so many games, early learned by these physicians, and they have resisted change since it affected their bank accounts." Stanley said. "When the government is involved in reimbursement such as Medicare, it makes rules that must be followed. Same with obamacare which expands its influence over a greater number of people and health care issues."

Jillian had sat quietly listening her father's explanation. "I heard today on the news, well Fox really, that president Obama's credibility is being questioned, and a recent pole showed that over 70% of Americans have lost faith in his judgment, because of obamacare and all of the lies he has told." She said.

"Makes you wonder who the 30% are who believe in him and why. Actually," he added, "a portion of the 30% have no opinion. How can people have no opinion?" Stanley responded.

"I also heard that with the New Year approaching, people are beginning to panic, since they have no idea if they will still have health insurance." Jillian said.

"The government has purposely lied to the American public and continues to downplay the fact that over 6 million families have had their health insurance cancelled. This could mean that it really involves over 18 million people. Obama continues to overplay the number of people 'enrolled', but we have received no real documentation of who really has insurance and how many of them are the young people needed, and how many are enrolled in Medicaid. Come the third of January, it will hit the fan when people are turned away by doctor's offices, have no access to their prescriptions and face huge bills if they go to the hospital." Stanley said as he rose to stretch.

"And of course," he added, Obama and the rest of the democrats will blame Republicans and make the insurance companies the bad guys."

"According to Fox, many democrats are defecting." Jillian said.

"They are in a panic because they know, now that their blind support for the president and his terribly destructive policies will give the public reason to toss them out on their asses in November of next year." Stanley said. "It's late and I have had a long day. I plan a shower, and Jen, turn my electric blanket on if you will."

TWENTY

The Essay

With three days remaining in which to complete her essay, Jillian collected all of her notes, and began to type the information onto the new Apple computer her parents had bought for her birthday. She had decided to present both a computerized and hand written version. Once she had entered a newly revised outline, she remembered that there were still some issues that she wanted to discuss with her brother Mark.

Jillian noted that the time at the top of her screen indicated that it was already 10 pm. She had been at it since seven, when they finished dinner. Mark's cell phone had rung four times when he answered it. She inquired if she had got him at a bad time, but he indicated that he had just sat down to relax after a light dinner.

"How's sort of married life, big brother. I understand that you have moved in with Karen." She laughed. "That must be great fun."

Mark looked around to make sure that Karen was still in the shower, and whispered into the phone. "Right. Not certain how long that will last." He said wearily.

"You two at odds again. I really like Karen and hoped that this was it." Jillian said. "What now?"

"You know that I am insured for liability, but not health by the hospital. "I checked into plans offered through the state exchanges and that abominable website on which I spent wasted hours, and ultimately found that my premiums would be more than doubled and get this, my deductible would be six thousand dollars. That means big money would have to spend, and that I don't have, before any insurance payment kicks in."

"So, what have you decided to do?" How does this create a problem between you and Karen?"

"When I told Karen that I had decided to pay the penalty at least for the first year, she went bonkers, telling me that it was my patriotic duty to buy health care. I think she was watching some of those Hollywood types videos, promoting this crap."

"Actually, I wanted to speak with you about insurance issues. Do you actually know any people who have been dropped by their insurance companies, and have been cost impacted, as you have?" Jillian inquired. "These are the missing pieces since I have heard MSNBC's version, and of course Sebelius' congressional testimony. Not to forget people on Fox like Alan Colmes who can find nothing bad about Obama, his policies in general or his health care."

"Suppose I email you the names of friends of mine and their families who have found themselves in the same situations. Would that work for you? Of course you won't use their real names. There are a number of attendings at the hospital, who have been dumped by insurance companies. Karen, Jillian's on the phone. Karen says hi, Jillian. Okay, she went back into the bedroom." Mark said softly.

"What are you going to do?" Jillian asked.

"As far as the insurance, I have to go naked, and take my chances that the hospital and my fellow docs will give me professional courtesy real big time." He paused. "As far as Karen, I just don't know what to do. When she gets her mind stuck on something, she is tough to be with. She cannot be my girl friend and my mother."

"What about wife?" Jillian asked.

"Simon says take ten giant steps backwards. I will email you the info as soon as we hang up. Love to Mom and Dad." He said.

Jillian went downstairs to print Mark's email when it arrived. Stanley asked about her progress in doing her assignment and suggested adding a bibliography of books and other resources she used for information. When her mother appeared with steaming cups of hot tea and home baked zucchini bread, Jillian told them of her conversation with her brother.

"I am worried about him. Without insurance. And from what I hear he could develop an ulcer, and they are not even married." Jennie said.

"I liked Karen as a person," Stanley said, "but I knew the moment I met her, that her chronic liberal attitude was not something that would go away even with a bit of enlightenment. It is a shame. But marriage? Mark has too many years yet to go without distractions such as Karen. It is too bad. But it is what it is."

"Perhaps you should speak with him." Jennie said.

"Mark is a big boy now. If he thinks he needs advice on affairs of the heart, he will ask." Stanley smiled. "I do not intend to butt in."A beeping noise emanated from the computer room indicating that an email had come in.

Jillian got up from the chair she was sitting on. "That's probably for me from Mark. He said he would send some info I asked about."

"So you have decided on a conclusion?" Stanley asked when she came back in with a number of printouts.

"I still plan to work it as a debate, taking both sides. I'll just look at the pros and cons and see which way it weighs out." Jillian said as she went back up the stairs.

Jillian spent about a half hour reviewing what her brother had sent, and then went back to her computer. She believed she was as ready as ever to begin. Jillian had shredded the outline she had shown to Ms. Davida Jones, having elected to work from a new one. She began her project with a preface:

'Since our class assignment, according to Ms. Jones has no limits as to words or paragraphs, I plan to provide both a computer printout of an essay that I alone have written, in addition to filling as many blue books, in my handwriting as needed, to complete the task. I will provide a list of all of the material used, that I reviewed, read from books and newspapers, information from the Internet, in addition to endless observations from television programs assumed to provide news in an unbiased fashion. Additionally, since the affordable care act is considered the underlying achievement of the individual about whom this essay is written, I have taken the time to listen to the opinions of many people in the medical profession.'

Jillian reviewed what she had written, and then referred to the actual wording of the assignment. She so wished to have Sasha here with her, but Sasha was undertaking efforts to fight her own demons. She sighed deeply and continued to type.

'The assignment was to provide information as to why Barack Obama, President of the United States, should be considered one of the greatest Presidents this country has ever had. I have decided to treat this as a debate where I shall take both the pro and con positions. It must be assumed that I shall erase any preconceived thoughts from my mind. Even those where I might have suggested that President Obama's likeness should be placed along those of other great Presidents on Mt. Rushmore.'

Jillian placed her arms behind her back and stretched. She took a deep breath and continued.

'Having decided to present the Pro position first, I looked at all of the accomplishments of this president. Not necessarily from the view of the White House, but what I have perceived since I am writing this essay. But before I deal with that, I find it imperative to discuss the promises, Barack Obama made during his effort to wrest the nomination from Hillary Clinton, neither of whom I perceive liked each other. The President's main slogan as seen from his posters, video promos and speeches was HOPE and CHANGE. While this was never clearly defined during this primary, one could assume that it was another well paid for campaign promise that most politicians might use when running for office. One must first understand that most politicians make promises they never intended to keep. As an aside I might suggest that politicians who are elected on such promises, should be held to them or recalled by the people who elected them.'

Jillian reread what she had written and smiled. Again referring to her outline, she was about to resume typing when her cell phone buzzed. Sasha wanted to know how she was doing. "I am on a roll." Jillian said.

"Me too," Sasha replied, "and it feels so good. See you in the morning. Sorry I bothered you."

Trying to recall her thoughts before Sasha's interruption, she smiled and continued.

'President Obama clearly stated just prior to his inauguration that he would "fundamentally change this country in the next few days."'

Jillian was not certain if that was his exact statement, but felt that his meaning was sufficient to include it.

Jillian decided to dwell on promises he made. 'The president advocated closing Guantanamo, ending the wars in Iraq and Afghanistan, having the most transparent administration ever, bringing the races together and working under an assumption that there were no red or blue states, only red, white and blue states. The latter suggested his intent to unify the country. The country had elected its first black president. And that was certainly a good thing. He, apparently was a Christian and attended church in Chicago on a regular bases, but had to distance himself from the minister of his church, Jeremiah Wright who often had presented sermons that evidenced racial bigotry, and what some might consider seditious statements against the country whose laws allowed him to speak as he saw fit. Although, in attendance on a regular basis, President Obama said never heard any of the angry dialogue.'

Jillian thought that she might remove that portion and save it for what might be considered a negative, but left it in place for the moment. She had barely made a dent in her assignment, when her mother knocked on the door.

Jennie entered the room. "It is almost midnight and you have school in the morning. Perhaps you should start a little earlier, darling."

Jillian yawned. "You are right as usual, Mom. I will brush my teeth and call it a night. Do you think Mark and Karen will break up?"

"Not for me to say, Jillian. Not for me to say." She kissed Jillian on the forehead and left the room.

TWENTY-ONE

Crunch Time

The next evening, after a dinner of hot dogs and sauerkraut, finished with chocolate ice cream topped with some of her father's pear preserves. Jillian was hard at work on her assignment. She decided to assign a point for each of the issues she would evaluate. The final decision would be based upon the number of credits or points accrued by each side of the debate.

'President Obama certainly was a principle in the decision to send a covert mission manned by Navy Seals into Islamabad to kill Usama bin Laden. Despite suggestions that he was also instrumental in delaying the mission, I have awarded him one point. With regard to removing our troops as promised from Iraq, he did so and deserves another point. We do not know, at this time whether, this decision to do so was based upon secure foreign policy or to placate members of his political base, but nevertheless, will award another point. To move ahead to the affordable care act, continuing to providing care for people with pre-conceived conditions will earn him a point, but this and allowing children up to their twenty-sixth year to remain on their parents health insurance companies will have to be re-evaluated later on. For now President Obama has earned four points for the pro side in this debate.' Jillian went down stairs for some lemonade.

"How are things going?" Stanley asked, as he put down book he was reading.

"They are going, Daddy." Jillian responded as she carried her drink back up to her room.

Jillian sipped some of her lemonade and then returned to her computer. She looked through her notes, and after finding nothing that served to augment the pro position, she began a new paragraph. Again, sticking to her newly revised outline that she had not shared with Ms. Davida Jones, she began a new paragraph entitled, THE OTHER SIDE OF THE DEBATE: Providing a negative response to the premise: 'Should President Barack Obama be considered one of the greatest presidents this country has ever had.'

'President Obama made a number of promises before and after he was elected. One of the promises was that his would be the most transparent administration this country ever had. History will show that this promise never ever came to fruition. Over a year ago, the administration watched and did nothing as four brave Americans were massacred by a group of terrorists in Benghazi. With regard to transparency, to date, America has not been told where President Obama, Vice-President Biden and Secretary of State Clinton were, what they knew, or what they were doing while Ambassador Stevens, his aide and two members of his security were murdered. Susan Rice was sent out to spread the "word" that it was a "spontaneous" response to a video. This has not been shown to be the case. Apparently the truth had it been known, might have reflected badly upon Obama's quest for re-election. The families of the murdered men are still looking for answers over a year after the terrorist attack took place. Another issue, unrelated, but also one that would put the president in a bad position, was the alleged low-balling of the unemployment figures in the months that preceded the election of 2012.'

'A new scandal surfaced when it became known that a gun running sting to Mexican cartels, allegedly instigated by the ATF, ran afoul when over a thousand guns were "lost" Unfortunately, at least one surfaced long enough to kill an American border patrol officer by the name of Brian Terry. The so-called investigation to date has provided little answers to the parents of the slain man. According to many what America got for answers, was obstruction and certainly not transparency.'

'A number of non-profit organizations had petitioned the IRS for relief granted to other similar organizations. It was reported that those organizations that might not have made contributions to the president's re-election campaign, or were considered pro Tea Party, or expressed adverse opinions about the policies of the administration, underwent more rigorous investigation, and experienced postponements of evaluation or complete denial. Obama put on an angry face, but certainly transparency never became part of the response. If my math is correct, this would give 4 points to the negative part of the debate.'

'The issue regarding the scope in which the NSA listens in on American's phone conversations remains debatable and might even be considered an essential factor in preserving national security. Certainly there are members of both major political parties that are at odds regarding this matter, but it has been ascertained that there has been no significant numbers provided where terrorist activity has been prevented. Certainly, even one instance might be well worth it, assuming the information is not used for political gain. I would call this a draw and assign no points to either side. The matter of foreign policy, and leadership will be summarized at the end.'

'Now we come to what is and will always be known as President Obama's signature legislation. In the year 2010, with a democratic majority in the House of Representatives and the United States Senate, the Affordable Care Act was passed. Unfortunately, to date, not one of the democrats who voted in favor of it have admitted to having read it. No House Republicans voted for it. The Speaker of the House at that time Nancy Pelosi of California, while not admitting to have read it, said that, "we would know what is in it once they passed it". With each passing day, the horrors associated with that statement have come back to haunt America, and hopefully those who voted for it.'

'By his repeated use of executive order, President Obama has defined, and redefined the law over and over again, to favor the Unions that contributed heavily to his re-election, and who expected big returns for their support. When it became apparent that the law was too restrictive and too cumbersome, the president made adjustments that he felt were politically expedient, with specific consideration regarding issues that could adversely affect the re-election of democrats in the 2014 midterm elections. This done despite how many Americans might be severely hurt by his convenient strokes of the pen.'

'On October 1, 2013, the website of all websites was rolled out, despite the alleged warnings of many, that doing so was premature, since it had never passed an acid test that suggested in any way that it could support any volume, or provide security that would protect any information provided by people finally able to access the website. It failed miserably and that failure was no surprise to people who wished it to fail, but more important, to knowledgeable people who have worked on similar software for years in the private sector. Should the fact that the company involved in developing the website was under the leadership of a woman who just happened to be a classmate of the wife of president Obama be suspect? I guess the definition of transparency once again has been parsed.'

'From my research, I have concluded along with many smarter and certainly more sophisticated than myself, that the impact on small businesses, the backbone of the middle class, and our economy, would be so severely impacted upon by obamacare, that its ability to recover is suspect. Having to cut both employment and working hours will not allow small businesses to grow. The president has given as much lip service to the need for jobs as he has his commitment to a good foreign policy. Case in point would be his appeasement of Iran. Yes, I have also reviewed the history of the Second World War. Look at the rewards of appeasement, and you will find so much evidence of "collateral damage", the loss of thousands of brave American soldiers, and a Holocaust that some would dare deny ever occurred.'

'Returning to the affordability of the law, it would appear that for so many, it is not at all affordable. With bizarre hype of lower premiums, will come unaffordable deductions, limited access to physicians and hospitals, and a decline in the quality of care. So what was the real intent behind a law that would be doomed to fail? Obama's agenda for a one-payer system has never been hidden from the voting public. Were they so busy collecting free money, free phones and free food to even think about what they were voting for? Apparently not. What President Obama provided over and over again, with regard to what we might expect regarding the care of our health were not promises. They were purposeful lies.'

'Unemployment is more of an issue than unemployment insurance, although the latter for a reasonable period is appropriate, assuming that it does not provide non-incentive for people to look for work. It has been apparent from everything that I have read about President Obama, that he is a socialist despite his many denials wishing to keep the people dependent.'

'This brings me to the conclusion of my essay. I, as well as many of my peers, will soon be of voting age. We all must ask ourselves what we would want for in a president. I would think that honesty, integrity, the experience and ability to lead, would represent just a minimum of our expectations. From all that I have researched, listened to, read and observed, the current occupant of the White House, fulfills none of the criteria. I truly believe that the big lie began in a Mombassa Hospital in 1961, and has been carefully hidden for all of the years that it took to groom and prepare someone to become the first black president of the United States. P.T. Barnum said that a "fool is born every minute". In light of the manner in which the American electorate has been deceived, Barnum was absolutely correct.'

'In response to the crux of the assignment and points awarded, in no manner should Barack Hussain Obama ever be considered among the greatest presidents this country has ever had.'

'Sources I have used: Books: "The Rise and Fall of the Third Reich, Obamanation, Dreams of My Father, Common Sense" and Current History Class Text: "The True History of the United States."'

'Media: MSNBC, NBC, ABC, FOX NEWS, CNN, NEW YORK TIMES, NEW YORK POST, LOCAL TOWN PAPERS, THE INTERNET'

'And lastly, conversations with family and friends.'

Jillian read everything she had typed into the computer, and printed three copies. Then she went about the tedious task of writing every word in the blue books provided.

TWENTY-TWO

Condemnation And Retribution

It was three thirty in the morning, when Davida Jones finished reading the essays, and she was livid, because she knew that she would be held responsible for not keeping her students in tow. Well aware that grants of government money was dependent upon delivering a consensus that would provide evidence that dollars already expended, were well spent if they motivated a significant number of high school students to accept, applaud, be motivated to influence their peers, and their parents to be more accepting of socialist programs, Davida Jones was appalled by what she had been reading for the past eleven hours.

Davida Jones moved away from a desk strewn with blue books and computer printouts, and quietly went to the room where her ten-year old son, Quinn still slept soundly. She watched the covers move with every breath, and then slowly closed the door and returned to her desk. Placing her head in her hands, she recalled that one time she forgot to ask her partner to use protection, so intent upon receiving the gratification she desired. Barely able to achieve a passing grade in her senior year of high school, she was able to attend an Indiana University, by the fruits of affirmative action, never once thinking that she might have displaced a more deserving candidate.

Now, she could be on the verge of losing everything, having guaranteed the Dean that she was assured her students would not dare to write anything that could jeopardize the grant the school needed so badly. She dreaded the confrontation that she would have with the Dean when school opened later that morning.

Later in the morning, before classes began, she waited in the Dean's outer office, with the blue books and computer printouts neatly piled on a table nearby.

The secretary looked up when her phone rang. She informed Davida that, the Dean had indeed arrived, and was in the parking lot. A few minutes past, when Dean Hannah made his appearance, and motioned for Davida to come into his private office. She declined an offer of coffee and went directly to the matter of the essays.

"Are you quite certain you do not wish some coffee? You look like you haven't slept." He observed.

"I have been up all night reading essays and you are not going to like the result." She responded.

"Give me the bad news, please." Hannah said.

She placed the essays on his desk. "The majority of the classes would not go along with the assignment as given, although there are a number who were either well indoctrinated or too frightened to get me angry." Davida said.

"Flunk the little bastards!" Hannah said spilling coffee over some of the material she had placed on his desk. "Shit! Shit! Shit!" He exclaimed, as he attempted to mop up the mess. Once most of the liquid had been absorbed, he returned to his seat.

"All of them?" She asked. "It would look bad, and I will have to somehow legitimize it."

"You said that they did not follow the assignment. That should be sufficient." He said.

"Perhaps, I could fail them on content or not providing bibliography. I will find something to justify my actions." She said.

"Do what ever you can, but be careful. Give them grades that will affect their acceptance to quality universities. Mix them up, but fail those you believe most deserving. I have appointments so take this mess off my desk. It is almost time for first bell. It is a good thing we decided to get rid of the pledge in the morning. Too time consuming, and you know what else." Hannah said as he rose and led her to the door.

The class sat quietly waiting for Davida Jones to begin. She looked up from her desk and frowned.

"For the most part, I am quite disappointed in your essays, and do not understand why you would write such horrible things about the president and clearly detrimental to your futures." She began, as Sasha and the rest of the class moved uncomfortably at their desks. They knew that this was an expected result, and although prepared, a great amount of uncertainty still remained.

Observing their discomfort, the teacher shrugged her shoulders and picked up one of the blue books. "Your grades will be determined by the manner in which you completed your assignment, grammar, information provided and making available, a source such as a bibliography." She said as Nancy Dick's hand shot up.

"Ms. Jones, you never mentioned a bibliography." Nancy said nervously.

"It is understood, when completing such a project as an essay assignment, one includes a bibliography, but you need not worry if your content is acceptable since it accounts for the majority of the grade." Jones remarked as she remembered that Dick's essay was more complimentary. "Also, I noted that some of you chose to work this as a debate. If you were not able to prove your case, there will be points deducted."

Sasha looked over to Jillian. They had indeed compared notes, and decided to use a debate to come to a conclusion.

Sasha raised her hand and was reluctantly recognized. "You gave us an assignment that had its conclusion embedded. That was wrong in the first place." She said.

"You and no one else ever complained, so it is a bit late to do so now. However, I believe the assignment was both clear and absolutely fair, considering that you are in a current history class." She gathered the books and print outs into a pile. "I will have your material graded by the day after tomorrow. In the mean time we do have a curriculum to follow. Your assignment for tomorrow is to read chapters fifteen through thirty in your text and prepare yourself for an exam to follow."

"That is an awful lot to read in one evening, Ms. Jones." Jillian complained. "We do have other school work, you know."

"Being rude will not gain you any favors regarding your essay grade which is already compromised." The teacher retorted angrily. If you are unable to do your work as assigned, and I see that that is already a problem, you will fail your test as well."

"Ms. Jones. What exactly do you mean by as well?" Sasha spoke up. "You said you have not yet graded our essays."

"As a teacher one gets a flavor and certainly an understanding of what a student is capable." Davida Jones said as she welcomed the ringing of the class bell. "You are all dismissed. No conferences." She added, noting both Sasha and Jillian approaching. "That goes for your two as well."

While Davida Jones was attempting to grade the essays in a way that Dean Hannah might find acceptable, he was on the phone trying to reach the members of the Board of Trustees that he believed he could count on for support. He was able to reach J. Evers Snoup, president of a local bank, easily enough at his club, the latter just having emerged from the steam bath and on his way to a massage with his more than favorite masseuse. Hannah had long ago found out that the J. never stood for anything, but could serve him as well as the S. in Harry S. Truman. It was immediately apparent from the conversation that Mr. Snoup did not handle adversity well, but Hannah reminded Snoup that he had always had defended him, particularly when the bank's books needed auditing, not to mention the times that Hannah had provided an alibi for the banker when his wife's suspicions of his improprietories surfaced.

The next call was made to Thornton Dick, whom he immediately reminded of his 'generous' donation to the politician's successful campaign for a state assembly seat. Dick was suspiciously evasive until, Hannah suggested that the essay his daughter Nancy submitted was more acceptable than most. He found it disturbing that Dick gave the impression of no more than lukewarm support for unexpressed reasons for the call. The Democratic Assemblyman was essentially noncommittal.

He had his secretary place a call to Malcolm Storey, but the Doctor was busy with patients and could not come to the phone. Hannah personally made three more calls to members of the Board he believed he could count on, but none of them provided any encouragement as to what to expect from other members, whom they had purposely kept out of the loop. So, of the twenty-one members of the Board Of Trustees, with the majority free of any known skeletons, Hannah began to develop a deep sense of insecurity. He thought briefly of calling Stanley Ashton, but he was not a member of the Board, and such a call might rouse suspicion.

Dean Hannah had Davida Jones called to the office at noon.

"I haven't had lunch yet, and never had breakfast." She complained as she took a seat.

"I did offer you coffee this morning." He reminded her. "But no matter, we have more important issues as hand." He went to the door, and opened it making certain that the secretary had gone to lunch, then closed and locked it. "We need a plan to offset any backlash from parents of students who get grades less than anticipated. It is after all the responsibility of academics to provide the best education. Is it not, Davida?"

She nodded her head. "What can we do?"

"It would seem to me that we just stonewall any suggestion that what we teach is politically motivated. After all, the standard has been set for years by educators at colleges and universities. A liberal arts education means just that." He thought for a moment. "Our texts are standard. That is correct?" He asked.

"We do purchase books from facilities that think politically as we, so they might be considered over the line by those on the right?" She responded.

"You mean those Tea Party idiots?" He bellowed. "They would never be treated with other than contempt by the members of the communities from whom most of our students come." His tone softened.

"Well, Sir, based upon what I am reading in these essays, we have a mini rebellion among select students. How their parents might feel is another issue." Davida said.

"Look, we live in a liberal stronghold. I truly believe that we will have the full support of the faculty, Board and parents once our position has been presented. That is if such might be needed." He responded.

"You really believe that most will be on board?" She asked.

"Even legally, what case could they possibly have?" He asked with a smile.

"I am no student of Constitutional law, but I might suggest some infringement on first amendment rights." She paused with a sigh. "And I am single parent and have too much to lose."

"We have enough legal clout on the Board as well as the school's attorney." He looked at Davida. "You are not even remotely contemplating backing down are you?"

Davida Jones was more frightened than she had been in a long time. "I am with you. I have no choice." She responded.

"Exactly," Hannah said, as he came around his desk to put his hand, heavily on her shoulder. "You actually have no choice whatsoever."

TWENTY-THREE

Intrigue

Stanley Ashton was upset with his daughter because she had not shared what had occurred in the classroom two days ago, but chose to just discuss their options after Jillian showed him the grade her essay had earned.

"What am I going to do now?" She asked with tears in her eyes. "I have to apply soon to colleges."

"First thing," Stanley said. "Is to understand that the law is on our side. Nevertheless, because of too many convenient associations in this community, we have to tread lightly and think everything out carefully. I would assume that some members of the Board, some members of the faculty, some parents and of course the Dean, feel quite assured that they are immune to any legal action. Let them think that way."

"But what can we do?" Jennie asked.

"Not panic." Stanley assured her. "Not panic at all." He thought for a moment, as he looked, again at the red D minus written on a card, provided by Davida Jones. "This is it? Where are your blue books? Should not your grade be imprinted on the essay? You do have a copy of the computer printout right?"

Jillian thought for a moment. "We always did have our essays or even tests returned with the grade marked on them. Why now is this different?" She asked. "Yes, Daddy, I saved the entire file on the computer."

"Great!" He said. "I want you to make a copy of the file on a USB and give it to me. It is dated correctly?"

"Of course," she responded. "That's done automatically. I will take care of that right now."

"What do you intend to do, Stanley?" Jennie asked.

"I have to think this out. But we should contact the people we know we can count on. Make a list with Jillian, but call Sasha and Kelly and arrange a meeting with just their parents for starters." He frowned. "I will call Thornton Dick and feel him out. Apparently his daughter Nancy received an unusually high grade."

"And Sasha and Kelly?" She asked. "How did they make out?"

"According to Jillian, Sasha got an F, but oddly, Kelly's grade was listed as 'to be determined'. Rather strange. Don't you think?"

Jillian had gone back to her room after dinner. She watched part of O'Reilly's memo and turned off the TV, when her iPhone's ring alerted her that Sasha was calling.

"How are you doing Jillian?" Sasha asked.

"I don't know, Sasha. I am starting to regret what I have done." Jillian replied.

"Do not, Jillian." Sasha pleaded. "We have done more to tell the truth than so many who will regret their inability to do so."

"But what about going to a school that might get you into medical school? You must have second thoughts." Jillian said.

"Actually, I don't. We have done the right thing. That is, of course, those of us who chose to be honest. Any idea as to what grades the others got?" Sasha said.

"Not absolutely certain, but Ms. Jones has always played favorites." Jillian responded.

"I have a feeling that what you said is not necessarily true. I think that Davida has received marching orders from those who are pulling her strings only with regard to kids whose parents might go along with all of this shit." Sasha said. "Right now your father is on the phone with my Dad. Have you spoken to Kelly since school?"

"I have not, but I do know that she got no specific grade as yet." Jillian said. "What do you suppose that means?"

"Well," Sasha answered. "Dr. Storey is on the school's Board of Trustees, even as a new member. Perhaps, the powers that be feel that a black man on their side would be an advantage."

"I don't believe that Kelly's father would do anything to disgrace her, no matter what the gain. He just has too much integrity." Jillian said.

"You are probably correct. I would think it best not to discuss this with Kelly." Sasha said.

"But, she is my friend as well as you are." Jillian implored. "We owe it to her to speak about what is going on."

"I suppose you are right." Sasha said. "But what do we really know about what is going on?"

"I plan to call Kelly now. She is too good a friend, and I believe that her father would not be a party to any kind of appeasement." Jillian said.

"Wait. My Dad just hung up from your father and he is speaking to Kelly's father now. I will let you know." Sasha said.

Sasha called back within minutes. "I just spoke briefly to Kelly. All she would say was that her father was livid."

"Livid about what. Her grade or your father's call?" Jillian asked.

"He is furious about her grade not yet determined, since he believes it is just another example of racism, but this time in reverse." Sasha said.

"Are you telling me that the school is trying to use her grade as a lever? He is after all a new member of its Board." Jillian added.

"Read into it any way you choose." Sasha added. "Your Dad will be getting a call soon about having all of the parents getting together for a meeting."

"The house phone is ringing. I'm going downstairs. I'll call you back if I have something to tell you." Jillian said.

"The shit is really going to hit the fan." Sasha said as she hung up.

Stanley spent twenty minutes on the phone with Malcolm and David, as both Jennie and Jillian listened to every word, wondering what was being said on the other two phones. It was clear that a meeting would be held for all parents who wished to attend.

"I hear you, David, but how can we even have an opinion about the Dick's girl's grade. Perhaps she went with the flow, and in the eyes of the teacher earned it. Yes, Malcolm. I agree that Kelly receiving a none grade or what ever that thing was called, certainly smacks of racial motivation." Stanley said.

Jillian tried to interject a comment, but Stanley waved her off as he continued to respond to the people on the other lines.

"I realize both of you are furious, but we will have to plan an attack with cooler heads. You must understand how angry I am for my daughter, and after all I feel some responsibility." Stanley said.

"No! Daddy! It was my essay and I believe everything I wrote. You have always taught me to be honest." Jillian cried out, as her father put an arm around her, hugging her to him.

"I agree, David. You start that rolling, and Malcolm, after you calm down, start making some calls. I plan to research historical revisionism in the morning when I get to my office." Stanley said, as he hung up.

"I can go with you to help." Both Jennie and Jillian said in one voice.

Stanley smiled and put his arms around both of them. "I appreciate that, but Jillian, you have to go to school tomorrow, and Jen, you are more needed at the unit than ever, to protect your patients from obamacare."

The class had assembled, and was in their seats about a minute before the last bell rang. Davida Jones had not yet arrived. Sasha got up from her desk to speak, when the door opened and a young woman they had never seen before entered and took a seat at the teacher's desk.

"My name is Barbra Sholde, and I am a substitute teacher for class today. Ms. Jones was called away on a family emergency."

"I just bet," Sasha muttered under her breath. "She doesn't have the balls to face us."

TWENTY-FOUR

Retaliation

A meeting was held, again, at the dance studio, where to David, Stanley and Malcolm's surprise, every student in the classes involved, had one or both parents present. Even Thornton Dick made an appearance, but was clearly more subdued, and did not exhibit his usual politically imposing self-sense of importance. Each individual wore a nametag provided to him or her upon arrival. The gathering was so large, that many resorted to sitting on the highly polished floor.

After an informal presentation by Malcolm, it was determined that Stanley would chair the proceedings again. It had been agreed upon by Stanley, David and Malcolm that the plan for the evening was to get a feeling from the group as to their understanding of what their children were being taught, and what texts were in the curriculum as required reading. Only after a sense was developed as to which if not all of the parents would give their full support, would Stanley and the others share the action the three had agreed upon. In their minds, Thornton Dick might still not be worthy of their trust.

To determine the extent of his cooperation, Malcolm rose to make a statement. "Stanley Ashton has agreed to act as attorney for this group should it be needed. This of course shall be pro bono. Therefore, you all will be asked to sign a paper that will provide attorney client privilege for your protection. I am certain that all of you have watched enough television programs to understand what that means. Additionally what we discuss here or one on one with you subsequently, should not be shared with anyone else, and that includes your children, if you are not assured of their complete compliance. If you feel unable to do this, now is the time to let us know."

After waiting a few moments, and since none of the group made any effort to leave, Malcolm continued. "I will turn the rest of the meeting over to Stanley."

Ralph Fineman appeared anxious. He was the owner of a local art supply store, and had always kept his political convictions to himself. Business was bad enough without degrading it further by angering some members of the close knit community.

"Exactly, what is the purpose of this get together?" He asked. Stanley looked over his reading glasses and saw that Fineman was not the only individual evidencing concern.

"An appropriate question," Stanley responded. "It is my assumption that all of us have concerns regarding the grading of an essay assigned to our children in the Current History class, but before we discuss that, I would like to query you on some issues regarding their education, that I hope cause as much concern to you, as it does to my wife and myself."

He looked at his notes for a moment. "I would like to know by a show of hands, how many of you know exactly what our children are being taught, and have looked at the texts that you have had to purchase for them." He paused to observe the response.

Of the individuals in attendance, ten put their hands up firmly, and five more initially responded but then weakly withdrew.

"Please understand, all of you, that the question is not meant to embarrass but to inform. God knows we all work very hard to pay for our children's education either by virtue of being able to send them to private school or public school, which is underwritten by our taxes." Stanley said as he looked for a response.

"Mr. Fineman. Excuse me. I know you as Ralph. Your daughter, Joyce has been a friend of Jillian since they were in kindergarten. Have you ever looked at any text Joyce has brought home?"

"Stanley," Fineman answered. "I work twelve hours a day and on weekends, in order to earn the money to keep her in school. We had hoped that Jason, our youngest, would be able to be enrolled in the academy next year. I have to admit that I have been remiss regarding how and what my daughter has been taught, but my wife Elaine has tried to keep up with it."

"I in no way wish to pick on anyone, since I am certain that some if not all of you can relate to what Ralph just shared with us." Stanley said, as he looked at David and Malcolm who nodded in agreement.

Luke Traumer stood up. "Look. It is all right for your three who probably earn more than the rest of us combined to pretend to be so virtuous. I too own a small business and am registered as a democrat just to keep it going, so my daughter Haley can stay in a good school. Why are you making these waves, causing trouble? I left my wife home in tears, when I told her I was coming here."

Malcolm looked at Stanley, who indicated he should say whatever was on his mind. "First, I will let you understand this. No one looks into my bank account and passes judgment unless he also will be willing to pay my bills. Many of those bills are for my wife's cancer treatment, which is something none of you ever want to deal with!" Malcolm swallowed hard, as Traumer sat down stunned by the revelation. "I am sorry, but it is what it is."

"Alright," Stanley said. "Perhaps we all need a bit of education as to what our children are being taught both in public and private school, since I full realize that many of you have children attending both."

"How many of you have gone on to college and or university, and earned degrees?" Stanley asked. With few exceptions many hands were raised.

Harris Shapiro asked, "So what? Now days degrees are useless, since the economy has tanked, and what ever we learned earns us nothing. I have a degree in engineering, but my firm went under when it became clear that it had no idea what the cost of health insurance might be. Look at all of those so-called IBM-ers who live among us. The difference there is that they had good pensions, forever for some. I have a daughter home hysterical, that she might not get into college because of some stupid grade on an essay, and an accident-prone wife who just fell again and broke her ankle and is in pain. I blame you Ashton for putting ideas into her head, that she should write an essay based upon conscience, and not just being damned practical!"

Stanley looked over his glasses trying to read the name pasted on the speaker's jacket. "Mr. Shapiro. I don't know who your daughter is and have never met her."

Harris Shapiro glared at Stanley. "She is friends with your daughter and his," he said gesturing at David. "You put all of these ideas in their heads, and I pay good, hard earned money to this school!"

"I told my daughter that if there was a problem, that I would have her back, as her father and as an attorney. It was never meant to go any further." Stanley said.

"Well, I guess it did just that." Harris said as he prepared to leave.

"Let me tell all of you that, as Malcolm has already explained, I am prepared to represent all of you, legally without charge if the need ever arises, and I will attest to that." Stanley responded.

David came forward, as Stanley gulped down some bottled water. "Look, we all have our axes to grind. We all have our crosses to bear. We all have our expenses to pay, and we all have to deal with an economy and a philosophy of education of which we all probably are terribly ignorant. We owe it to our children, to learn, not only what they are being taught, but why. This incident regarding the essay, and the reasons for the poor grades given by a teacher, whose motives are yet to be determined is what has opened our eyes. But, determine them we shall. And while we are doing just that, we will look into the rest of the curriculum that is being taught to our children, because, no matter how busy one might be or how frightened of reprisals, it is our duty to do so."

"I could not agree more with David," Malcolm said. "You all are obliged to do a little research. If you do not have computers where the Internet will provide an enormous amount of information, please go to your public libraries, where books and use of computers are also available. We can give you some starters, but Google has become so sophisticated, typing something such as, 'liberal or progressive school texts in question' might just be enough to work."

Both David and Stanley nodded in agreement, as David continued. "It is getting late and my wife has generously allowed the use of her dance studio for our meeting. I had better clean it up so we may use it again. We will let you know when."

Stanley took Malcolm and Thornton Dick, who had remained quiet, aside. "David and I would like to speak with both of you after everyone has gone." He said.

Thornton Dick appeared nervous as the three surrounded him. "Look, Thornton," Stanley said. "You are a member of the Board. I would like to have a look at the By-laws.

"Why would you require that? I am not certain that it would be appropriate." Thornton said nervously.

"If you are with us, there should be no problem. I know full well that your daughter received a better grade than most of the students. Was it your influence?" Stanley asked.

"Hannah contacted me last week to tell me that there was an issue and wanted to know how many of the Board members he might count on." Dick replied. "That was the last time I spoke with him. I do not want my daughter to suffer."

"Will you give me a copy of the By-laws?" Stanley repeated.

"I will if I am not considered a co-conspirator, and nothing more than a concerned parent." Dick responded.

"We will have no issue with that." Stanley said. "Suppose I drive home with you. I assume that you have a copy at your house, or is it at your office?"

"No, I don't keep any such documents in Albany. I will give it to you tonight." Dick responded.

"Great!" Stanley exclaimed. "That will be most appreciated by us, the current students at the Academy and all that follow."

TWENTY-FIVE

Sasha

David Finkel had left the house around four a.m., having been called in to attend an emergency Caesarian section, carefully closed the front door so as not to awaken Jelena or Sasha. Later that morning, when he arrived at his office in the old section of Kingston, he was surprised to find Sasha in the waiting room.

"Why are you not in school, young lady?" He asked.

"I needed to talk to you, so I called in sick, telling them it was Jelena." She responded.

"Well your mother certainly has a definite accent, so how did you pull that off?" David asked.

"She is not my mother!" Sasha said defiantly. "Any way, I am pretty good with accents. Can we talk, alone?" Sasha asked.

David escorted her into his private office, and asked her if she wished some coffee. She declined stating that she had breakfast. "How did you get down here?" He asked.

"I took Kenny's car." She said. "He was still asleep. I left him a note."

"Your brother will have a fit, and your learner's permit clearly shows, you must have a licensed driver with you."

"I am a good driver, and I was very careful." She responded.

This was not the first time David Finkel's strong willed daughter had defied him, and she was the reason why he left a lucrative private practice in Livingston, New Jersey for a new life in upstate New York, where the cost of living was higher and the politics more suspect. Not to forget the absurd New York taxes on gasoline. He also left a five thousand square foot home where the property taxes were six times the cost of the house he grew up in Woodbridge, New Jersey. He received his Bar mitzvah in a conservative temple there, where membership had dwindled to a point, that it had been sold and converted into a veterinary hospital.

After high school, he attended a college in New England on a variety of scholarships, and graduated Cum Laude to the delight of his parents, who sold their home, in order to pay for his tuition in medical school. After residency and a two-year stint in the army, he joined a small pediatric practice in Livingston, New Jersey where he decided to make his home. David met his wife Amy, who was an emergency room nurse at St. Barnabas Hospital. Amy gave birth to their son Kenny in 1994 and Sasha in 1997. Four years later in 2001, soon after the terrorist attacks on the Twin Towers, Amy died of breast cancer.

Presented with the task of raising two young children, and having to devote a reasonable amount of time to his pediatric practice, David advertised for an au pare to take care of Kenny and Sasha. Although only twenty-four years of age Jelena impressed David enough for him to hire her. He fell in love with her and despite the ten-year difference in their ages, they married in 2004. Sasha would not accept her and became disruptive. After a year of group therapy, David felt strongly that the family should move, and finding an opportunity in Kingston, New York, he relocated to Saugerties. Sasha, over time, seemed to adjust, but refused to call her stepmother anything but Jelena. In an attempt to find something with which to occupy her time, Jelena started her small studio in town, having attended dance school in her former country.

David sat back in his chair. "Okay, Sasha, what's on your mind?" He asked.

"I am concerned about my grades. I am concerned about getting into college and I am concerned about my future." She sighed. "I am not sure we did the right thing."

"With regard to what you wrote?" He asked.

"No!" She asserted. "I believe in what I wrote. I am concerned what you all plan to do, and if it will make things worse."

"What we plan to do, Sasha, is to call a Town Meeting of the School, where all of the parents and students who wish to, can have their say about things that might think troublesome. Now I am sure that Jillian's father has already told her about that, but it is not to be broadcasted yet, right?"

"You know you can depend upon me, but what do you hope to accomplish?" She asked.

"Stanley Ashton believes we can apply enough reasonable pressure on the Dean and the Board to take a hard look at what has transpired, and change your grades." David said.

"Is that legal?" She asked.

"Stanley is a good lawyer. Enough said." He replied. "Now, I have until eleven til my first patient, so I'll drive you home and have your brother take me back to the office. After all you must need some rest for this sudden illness requiring your absence from school. And I will give you a doctor's note." He smiled and gave Sasha a hug. "Try not to be too hard on Jelena. I loved you mother, but Jelena makes me happy and she is my wife, after all."

TWENTY-SIX

Jillian

After dinner, Jillian asked to speak with her mother and father about issues regarding what had transpired at school. Similar to Sasha, she was conflicted about what might result from the coming town meeting she heard her parents discuss during dinner, but not about the conclusion she had come to, with regard to her essay.

"I believe in what I now believe in, having had to admit how duped I had been about the president, and how foolish I feel that I so easily accepted everything he said. Well just about everything. I am worried that there are so many young people in denial who could, in my way of thinking, misuse the privilege of voting in the next presidential election." She said.

"I can't tell you how much we admire you for what you just said." Stanley remarked. "I have no trepidation about fall out from the town meeting since I am confident we will prevail. I plan in my presentation to discuss the state of education in general, in both the public and private schools, and the lack of balance as to what is taught, the texts that are used, the basis upon which teachers are hired, and the misuse of tenure, when so called educators are called to task." Stanley said.

"But do you know if you are on safe ground to even call a town meeting at the school. It is a private institution." Jennie offered.

"Darling, you know me better than to go into something like this without being assured of the end result." Stanley picked up a thick manila folder that he had earlier been thumbing through.

This afternoon, I read all one hundred and five pages of the By-laws of the Agnes Endicott Witherspoon Preparatory School, and on page 92, it clearly states that town meetings are to be held at least once every year, and that an additional meeting may be requested by any member of the Board who deems it imperative."

"I don't recall going to any town meetings." Jennie remarked.

"You are absolutely correct, Jen. There has not been a meeting called at least during the few years Jillian has been a student. Malcolm is newly appointed to the Board. Thornton Dick, now is another issue, and should have known better, had he read the By-laws. He has admitted that he has not." Stanley said as he flipped the papers he held in his hands.''

"Where did you get that from, Daddy?" Jillian asked.

"I promised in all confidence that it would not get out unless the individual who gave it to me chose to say so."

"It was Nancy Dick's Dad. Wasn't it?" Jillian asked.

"I shall neither confirm or deny." Stanley said.

"Than I shall assume that Jillian's astute assumption is correct, and I applaud him for doing so." Jennie said. "I must remind you that I have been living, happily with an attorney for let's see an umpteen number of years." She laughed as she hugged her husband.

"So what's to do next?" Jillian asked.

"We have Malcolm call for an immediate town meeting." Stanley answered.

"Why not Thornton Dick?" Jennie asked. "He has been on the Board for a longer period of time."

"We don't wish to put to much pressure on him right now. I really believe that he is at his turning point. I would like to see a member of the Democratic Party reject policy in favor of principle. He might even be the poster boy for a Democratic Party free of deceit and partisanship, willing to favor country over party." Stanley said.

"Don't hold your breath!" Both Jennie and Jillian said in unison.

"I am prepared to take any crumb that might lead to a whole loaf." Stanley responded.

"Our daughter does not seem totally convinced." Jennie said as she observed Jillian.

"As much concerned I am for my future I am troubled my peers will have to shoulder all of this debt that the government has accrued. What do they care! When the Senators and Congressmen and women are allowed retire to some cushy existence, because of all of the graft and payoffs they believe they have 'earned', while the rest of the young people will have to shovel themselves out of all of the so-called 'shovel ready crap'. This president and his administration and the congress, believe themselves so entitled to the many excesses, both legal and illegal, that our generation will have to pay for. Yes, Daddy, I read all of the books you suggested and many more."

"I am momentarily speechless, and for an attorney, that is the most demeaning admission one could make. Is there an answer? Yes, there is. A fair and balanced, unbiased submission of the facts presented by all parts of the media from which young people like you can make appropriate decisions. Bottom line. Clean out Washington and start fresh." Stanley said.

"Don't forget the need for educators to act accordingly." Jennie said.

"I have not forgotten that at all, but again, I suggest you don't hold your breath, until we can have at least some control at private schools, over the curriculum, the people advancing it and their agenda. Lots of work to do." Stanley said.

"So what is next?" Jillian asked.

"You all go to school as usual. Attend all of your classes. Try not to sass your teachers. Best behavior should be the mantra, so pass it on. In confidence, Malcolm Storey will call for a meeting later this month, and as there are two weeks left in the year, he will meet the criteria of two week notice, that is according to these By-laws that no one seems to adhere to." Stanley said.

"What do you mean?" Jennie asked.

"Suffice it to say, there is much written here that has not been followed, but I will not deal with that now, but certainly later on. It is apparent that too many Board members enjoy perks, but not the work they are required to do to 'earn them'."

TWENTY-SEVEN

Panic

When Roland Hannah received the frantic call from Murray Gannif, that Malcolm Storey had requested a town meeting, he turned beet red and began to perspire.

"Who does he think he is to meddle in school affairs?" Hannah said angrily. "Further more, what right does he have to do this? You're a lawyer, Murray. Do something about this!"

"Actually," Gannif responded. "As a member of the Board of Trustees, he has every right, according to the By-laws."

"I knew it was a mistake to make him a member!" Hannah said.

"As I recall, Roland, it was you who wanted him on the Board, for what I believe you called diversity."

"Well, never mind about that, since it is water under the bridge. What can we do now?"

"We allow the meeting to happen. Try to make the date and time inconvenient for most people." Gannif said.

"Like during school hours, I think would be the best time. How long can we put this off?" Hannah asked.

"We are obligated to set the date two weeks from the day requested." Gannif said.

"How about a Sunday, early, then?" Hannah said.

"Don't be a fool, Roland. They will see right through that." Gannif answered. "We can't stall them."

"We had better get our people together, and on the same page. How many can we depend upon for support?" Hannah asked. " But, I have to see some disgruntled parents now about the food served in the cafeteria. Could it be that bad?"

"How would I know? I have never eaten there. Have you?" Gannif asked.

"Actually no. But I have walked through the area during lunchtime. None of the teachers have complained, but then, again, they bring their own lunch and eat in the faculty room." Hannah said. "Do what you can to stall this. Don't forget the grant!" The attorney said he would see what he could do and hung up.

About an hour later, while Stanley was on the phone with Jennie, a beep notified him of an incoming call.

"I'll get back to you later, Jen." He said he took the new call.

Malcolm Storey was on the other end. "All of this intrigue is biting heavily into patient care." He said. "I just ended a half hour conversation with Murray Gannif. You know he is on the Board."

"Better known as 'Ambulance Chasing Murray The Goniff'." Stanley said. "A purposeful play on a Yiddish word for thief. I know him well and not fondly."

"Well, he tried to get me to postpone the town meeting beyond the two week period required." Malcolm advised.

"And for what reason?" Stanley asked.

"Something idiotic, like the Board was not prepared to call a meeting at such short notice. I told him that I called the meeting, and had a perfect right to do so." Malcolm said.

"So, what was his final answer?" Stanley asked.

"He relented, but wanted to schedule it at a time when it would not be feasible for all to attend, and as we have discussed we want as many children as well as parents there as possible."

"And when did he propose the meeting could be held?" Stanley asked.

"The night of the big basketball tournament." Malcolm replied, but I told him that it would be held two weeks from yesterday on Wednesday night at seven, and in the auditorium which will seat three hundred."

"I am sure he liked that." Stanley said.

"Obviously not. He fumed. Called me a few choice words that I plan to remind him of, and said that he would discuss it with the Dean and other Board members. I also took the liberty of telling him that, not following the Biy-laws would encourage a complete investigation of the Board, more than likely followed by litigation if need be." Malcolm said.

"You did well. The town meeting will occur, and the presence of the Dean, the faculty and all of his co-conspirators on the Board will be attending." Stanley said. "Whom on the Board can we depend upon?"

"I think we can depend upon at least fifteen of the twenty-one members, but I am not certain about our good buddy Thornton Dick." Malcolm offered."

"I think he will come around, actually." Stanley said. "Good job on your part."

"Thank you very much. Now I hope I can let this rest until a week from Wednesday and que sera, sera. I really must get back to the business of patient care." Malcolm said, as the conversation ended.

TWENTY-SEVEN

The Town Meeting

Much to the dismay of Dean Hannah, and certain members of the Board and the faculty, the auditorium of the Endicott-Witherspoon Preparatory school was filled to capacity, with folding chairs brought in for additional seating. There were no signs, and the audience of adults, school children and their siblings sat quietly waiting.

Long tables had been placed side by side to accommodate the Board of Trustees as well as members of the administration and teachers, who had been specifically asked to attend. At a table off to the side of the stage and perpendicular to the one reserved for the Board, Dean Hannah, Davida Jones, Murray Gannif, Edgar Fluecke and Vernon Jarretts sat quietly. A podium had been placed down on the floor of the auditorium, near the edge of the stage.

Reid Harris, the current president of the Board whose term was due to expire, walked onto the stage and approached Hannah, Gannif and the teachers. He leaned over to Hannah and smiled. Then he took his seat at the table designated for the Board. Cards bearing the names of each member had been prominently placed in front of each seat. One by one members of the Board filed in from a door to the right of the stage, led by Thornton Dick, who then occupied the seat to the right of Harris. The last to arrive and be seated was Dr. Malcolm Storey who had been placed at the furthest end of the table. Hannah and Harris frowned, as a smattering of applause from the audience greeted Malcolm.

When the audience had quieted down, Hannah presented open palms to Reid Harris, suggesting that he begin.

Harris cleared his throat and looked at Stanley Ashton, who sat in the front row with Jennie, Jillian, David and Jelena Finkel, and Sasha. Kelly Storey sat behind them with her mother. Stanley had saved seats for Mark and Karen, but he ultimately arrived without her.

"I must say that the sudden need for calling this town meeting is quite unorthodox, and I must add seemingly unnecessary. However, that said, we are here to conduct business, or what ever it is that upsets or offends certain parties." He paused to clear his throat. "Alright, Dr. Storey, since this was your idea, why don't you start!"

Malcolm Storey walked to center stage. Kelly Storey called out, "Go Doc!", as Reid Harris raised his hand for silence.

"Actually, there are many of us, both parents and students concerned with how and what are children are being taught." He looked down at Stanley. "I believe that Stanley Ashton will be the first to speak." He glanced at Murray Gannif. "May I ask why you are not seated with the rest of the Board?"

Ganniff looked up from a conversation he was having with Hannah. "I am representing the Board as an attorney."

"Looks more like you are representing the Dean and some of the faculty!" Bob Logan called out from the back of the auditorium.

Malcolm shielded his eyes to see who had just spoken. "Everyone will get a turn to speak who wishes to do so." He said. "Some one give me a hand to bring the podium up here on the stage, so the speakers can be seen." Harris Reid was about to protest but thought better of it, as Stanley, Mark and Dave Finkel lifted the wooden podium up onto the stage.

"We will need a microphone as well, hooked up," Stanley said.

Once everything was in place, Stanley Ashton walked up the stairs to the stage and stood at the podium. He first made certain that everyone in the auditorium could hear, and then introduced himself.

He looked at Reid Harris, who was having a conversation with Thornton Dick. "I hate to interrupt you Mr. Harris but in response to orthodoxy, your By-laws stipulate that there shall be one Town Meeting each year. We have only two weeks left before we will be wishing everyone Happy New Year, and no meeting had been called except for this one, and only at Dr. Storey's request."

"May I ask how you obtained a copy of our By-Laws?" Harris asked, noting what Ashton had brought with him.

"Why every member of the Board has a copy, I believe. Is the public to be denied as well?" Murray Ganiff started to protest, but Stanley ignored him. "I assume that what is contained in the By-Laws of the school many of our children attend, is not considered secret, nor should the administration and the Board be considered clandestine operations. Am I right?" As no one responded, he continued.

Hannah whispered into Gannif's ear. "Say something or object! You are a lawyer!"

"Desmond," Gannif responded, "This is not a court and unfortunately, he is correct, so far."

Stanley overheard the aside and smiled. "There are a number of issues that have to be addressed." He observed Jeanette Pelochi, the Treasurer and Secretary of the Board, whom he knew he would not count on for support, look at her watch. "And we plan to stay until every issue has been presented, and every person who wished to speak has done so."

From the back of the hall, someone called out, "I'll drink to that!" Noting Father Anthony, Pastor Joe and Rabbi Tom standing near the door, he said softly to himself, that he hoped the comment had not come from any of them, with his hand covering the microphone.

Despite the fact that the lights in the auditorium had not been dimmed, no one noticed Bob Logan approaching the side of the stage. "I'd like to know on what criteria my daughter was failed on her essay, along with so many of her classmates! That's what I want to hear from Ms. Jones!" He called out, as David Finkel took him by the arm and gently pushed him down into the seat Stanley Ashton had occupied.

Davida Jones started to push her chair away from the table. "I'm not sitting around for any of this." She told Murray Gannif, who grabbed her arm, keeping her from rising.

"Stay where you are, Davida. Don't give any of them any reason to think you have done anything wrong." He advised. "We have gone over all of the possible questions they might ask. Just respond to them as we have rehearsed." Davida relaxed and leaned forward, her hands clasped on the table.

Reid Harris asked that there would be no more outbursts from the audience in any form, including applause.

Stanley moved closer to the podium where he had placed his papers, despite the fact that he did not require any notes. "Bob Logan's query brings me to my first issue, that of the assignment, and since Ms. Jones is the teacher who assigned it, I will address my remarks to her." He turned to the table where the teacher sat nervously. "What was the purpose of assigning the class an essay whose topic left nothing for debate of any kind?"

David Jones squirmed and looked at Hannah and Gannif. The latter extended his palm as to say, 'answer the man's question'.

"I though it would be a good exercise in civics, she said, softly."

Stanley walked over to where she was sitting, taking the microphone with him. "I doubt if any one heard your answer. You have such a soft voice. Please, we can share the microphone." He said, as she repeated her answer, hesitantly. Some members of the student body snickered.

"We do have audio visual facilities. Do we not?" Stanley asked, as Dean Hannah nodded in the affirmative.

"I thought so, since I have been here for presentations that required an ample number of microphones as well as speakers." Stanley said.

Dean Hannah quickly rose from his chair almost upsetting the pitcher of water in front of him. "If some of you had not seen the need for this rushed town meeting, we would have been better prepared!" He bellowed.

Stanley smiled. "You are telling me that two weeks and a day was not enough time to manage that? One would think that poor acoustics might make some of your answers more difficult for the audience to hear."

Gannif pulled Hannah back into his seat and whispered something into his ear. "We can provide better audio now if that is your wish." Hannah said to Stanley.

"Very gracious of you, Dean." He turned toward the audience." Anyone feel that they cannot hear what people up here are saying?" He asked.

"If they speak up and not mumble, we shall hear just fine." A voice said from the back of the auditorium. Stanley smiled, recognizing Father Anthony's distinct baritone.

"Now that we have resolved audio, Ms. Jones, why did you feel that the best topic for an essay that would count two thirds of the grade for the semester, would be the one you chose to assign?"

Before he put the microphone in front of her, Stanley looked at a paper he held. "I want to be exact." He said. "Why you believe that Barack Obama should or will be considered the best president this country ever had? That is correct yes?"

Davida nodded. "Did everyone in the audience see that Ms. Jones answered in the affirmative?" Stanley asked.

Gannif got up and hit the table. "This is not a court of law, Ashton, so stop treating it as one." He yelled.

"Sorry you see it that way. You will get your turn as well." Stanley responded and turned back to Davida Jones. "Okay, so why did you choose to assign an essay that based upon how you worded it, could only be answered in one way. Did it ever occur to you that there are people in this country who may not believe what you believe?"

"Since I am the teacher of a Current History class, it was perfectly reasonable to do so." She said emphatically, as Dean Hannah nodded his approval.

"Fine, let's go beyond that now. The class or classes, as a whole, completed the essay, and handed it in typed as well as hand written in the blue books. I am correct?" He shoved the microphone in her face.

"That is correct," she responded.

"Let's get to the manner in which the essays were graded. You did read and grade all of them yourself. Correct?" He asked.

"Yes," she responded wearily.

"Assuming that all of the i's were dotted and the t's crossed and grammar was reasonably correct, and everything was received by you in time, what determined an A and what determined an F as a grade?" He paused. "Actually, there weren't any A grades were there?"

"No!" She said angrily. "None deserved an A".

"But you did give one of the students a B or B-. Am I correct?"

She knew he was referring to Nancy Dick. "Yes."

"And that was based upon what?" Stanley asked.

"I don't recall," she answered. Stanley observed Thornton Dick's face turn red.

"Okay, now I am going to embarrass my own daughter Jillian and her friend Sasha Finkel, and yes Tara Logan, for starters." He looked down into the audience at Bob Logan.

"All three of those students I mentioned received failing grades. Is that not correct, Ms. Jones?" Stanley asked.

"I don't remember." Davida said, looking at Gannif for help.

"Stop harassing a teacher as qualified as Ms. Jones." Gannif admonished.

"Glad you brought that up, Murray." He turned to Davida again. "Let's talk about your qualifications. "Might there ever have been issues with your high school grades, that could have prevented you from going to college or a college of your choice?" Stanley was on a fishing expedition.

"That is an extraordinary misuse of the reason for having a town meeting?" Gannif objected.

"No, Mr. Gannif." Davida Jones said. "I can answer that question. I want to answer that question. My high school grades were not great, but our government afforded me the way to attend a quality college. So don't lecture me, Mr. Ashton as to how it feels not to be able to get a good education" Both Hannah and Gannif sucked in air.

"I see," Stanley said. You are speaking about affirmative action, where it is conceivable you might have taken the place of some one with a higher grade point average. If you wish understand how upset your classes are because of the grades you handed out, I ask you again, on what basis did you make the determination of what grades to give?" The hook was out.

"They did not respond appropriately to the assignment and some said terrible things about the president and his policies." She said, as Reid Harris groaned. He had the imaginary gavel but dared not to use it. Members of the Board leaned forward to grasp every word, and some seemed very upset from what they were hearing.

Bill Klein, who had been a member of the Board for five years, and whose children had graduated from the school a few years ago, asked the Chair if he might ask a question. Stanley brought him the microphone.

"You can hold on to that thing. Lord knows, everyone in this place will hear me loud and clear." He looked at Davida Jones. "Are you telling us that if people do not agree with your political views and vomit them as taught, back to you, in whatever form, you will fail them?" Before she could answer, he persisted, looking at Dean Hannah. "Hannah, is this true of all of the faculty, you encouraged us to sign off on?"

Hannah's collar was soaked with perspiration, and the two Martinis he had at dinner did not help at all. He was about to provide some feeble response, but Klein had already turned back to the embattled teacher.

Harris Reid banged the table with his hand. "Let's have some decorum here, and not frighten the students. Bill, we have graduated students with honors and they have gone on to some great colleges and universities."

But Klein persisted. "Really. I would be even prouder of that fact if I was assured that their grades were earned, by the courage of their convictions, and not from either being extorted or brainwashed. I was very liberal in my youth, but I grew up and became more conservative. In my day, we had some tough teachers, but if we were given both sides of a story, we were able to draw our own conclusions. Our grades were based upon our ability to provide enough information that could prove our point. We did not have to agree with everything the teacher taught to get a decent grade. Unfortunately, from what I have been hearing from my grandkids in college, this is no longer the case. What the hell is wrong with the education provided in this country and the educators that provide it? And don't give me any of that claptrap about throwing more money in. God knows we have done that, and it just doesn't work. We need an unbiased faculty. No more tenure. And as a member of this Board, I will be the first to ask for the resignation of anyone not up to snuff and that is not limited to the faculty!"

"What about the grades?" Selma Morton cried out. "My daughter was too embarrassed to come. What about the grades."

Stanley walked over to edge of the stage. "Selma. That will be dealt with, but not tonight."

"Grades cannot be changed without good reason!" Dean Hannah hissed, as Gannif pursed his lips.

"Ah," Stanley sighed. "Good reason. Yes. We will get to that. Murray, you took some of the steam from my message."

Jeanette Pelochi rose from her seat, and asked for the microphone. Members of the Board who had always believed she did not belong there shuddered at the thought of her speaking. "Teachers must be respected for their decisions. They after all have followed the curriculum to which no parent, I am aware of, has objected. After all the Board passed on the year's curriculum that certainly included the Current History class's teaching objectives."

Thornton Dick said. "I never saw this year's curriculum," and five other Board members echoed his thought.

"Well", Pelochi said. "It was passed at last meeting of last year. It was passed unanimously actually." She added.

"Wait a minute," Dick said. "I recall an eleventh hour vote on some matter, the Chair, here said was routine. I must admit I never read it, and am saddened by my negligence."

"He should keep his mouth shut," Davida Jones whispered to Gannif. "I gave his daughter Nancy a good grade."

Thornton Dick grimaced at the remark.

"That, Assemblyman Dick, as you know from your dealings in Albany is business as usual." Pelochi had difficulty smiling, the skin around her mouth appearing unusually taut. She also never seemed to blink her eyes. "I have always said that only after you legislate a matter will you come to understand what it is all about."

"Dumbest thing I have heard all night!" The voice again came from the back, and everyone knew it was Rabbi Tom.

Thornton Dick looked at her in amazement. At that moment, Stanley, Malcolm and David knew they could depend upon another member of the Board.

Stanley took back the floor. "I have, also, a few words to say about education, and can certainly understand why Bill Klein expressed himself the way he did. But before I go there, I have some questions about textbooks. First from parents in the audience."

He walked to the edge of the stage. "Be honest now. How many of you parents have looked at or read any of the texts, your children are assigned?" Stanley raised his hand, but few hands rose from the audience. How many of you discuss their homework on a daily basis or what goes on in school" Many hands went up. "That's good, because all of us pay premium dollars to have our children educated, but I believe we all, tonight have received an education that is most disconcerting."

Stanley returned to the podium and referred to his notes. "Textbooks and educators have the ability to distort history for political and propaganda purposes. There seems to be a disturbing pattern with regard to religion as written in many current history texts. We no longer have anything resembling civics taught in school, and seem to diminish Judaic/Christian accomplishments, while promoting those of Islam." He looked back down at his notes.

"It seems that with the rise of liberalism and something that Theodore Roosevelt and Woodrow Wilson promoted, called progressivism, such things as school prayer, and even the pledge to the American flag have been eliminated." Stanley said.

Murray Gannif got up and joined Stanley at the podium, taking the microphone from its stand. "We did not come here to hear a speech. Did we?" He looked at the audience.

"I think we are learning more tonight than we have in the past two semesters," A female voice came from the second row. Jillian looked behind her and saw Sasha with a big grin on her face. She started an applause that built throughout the entire auditorium. Gannif reluctantly went back to his seat, after dropping the microphone onto the podium with a loud thud.

The audience quieted down, and Stanley took that as a sign they wished him to continue. "The bias projected in some of the texts children in this country must use as reference and sources of history is deplorable. There are forces around and among us attempting to make this a country devoid of religion. Pilgrims are depicted as without any religious life, completely changing without any sense of reality what some of older folks and not so older folks learned when we were the same ages of our children. When were we ever taught that the first Thanksgiving was meant for the Pilgrims to thank the Native American Indians and not God for bounty received? Who conceived, other than Hitler to remove the contributions made to science by the Jewish people from some textbooks? There are too many other examples to comment on." No one rose to object."

Stanley continued. "The costs of publishing school texts have risen extraordinarily. Do you realize that only three publishing houses control the minds of our children from K to 12? And they are located in Texas and California."

He had the complete attention of the audience. "I should think better of Texas, but have little expectations from California, where nothing good seems to emanate. Now I believe that bad history can lead to bad policies. The distortion of history is a ploy used by every oligarch, every totalitarian and fascist. Hitler had Goebbels to spew his propaganda. Every politician, in his own way does the same. We need history reported as it occurred and not changed to suit some ideological agenda. History can shape a nation's identity, its culture and certainly for many, provide memories both good and bad. That is the history our children deserve to be taught."

He waited for the applause to die down, and then asked if anyone from the audience would like to speak. Ganiff started to speak, but Bill Klein took the liberty of waving him down.

Jelena Finkel rose slowly, and raised her hand. "I would like to." She said, as David Finkel led her up the stairs to where Stanley waited.

TWENTY-EIGHT

Jelena

"My name is Jelena Finkel, the wife of Dr. David Finkel and the mother of Sasha, but I guess you know all that." She grabbed David's hand as he was about to leave the stage, but he whispered that she would be just fine, and to speak into the microphone.

"I hope you can understand me. My English may not be so terrific even though I have lived her in this great country for many years now. I was born in Croatia when it was still part of Yugoslavia, and was but a teenager when the civil war broke out. War is terrible for both the good and the bad, but we were grateful when then President Clinton, intervened. Bad blood remains, still inflamed by some, in the name of religion. I came to this country, learned its language, and I was thrilled to assimilate into its culture, without forgetting where I came from."

Jelena looked at Sasha and her husband both of whom had broad smiles on their faces. "I come with no notes, no script and obviously no teleprompter." The latter caused laughter from the audience, and frowns from Dean Hannah and Davida Jones.

"When I found a place to stay with people I knew from the old country, I got a job in what you call a fast food restaurant, slinging burgers. It was a small job but we all have to start somewhere, and this country provides so much opportunity for those who seek it out. When I could afford it, I took a bus ride to Washington D.C. and was astounded by all of the huge white buildings and the statues built to honor the people whose contributions made this country great."

"I saw the Declaration of Independence and the Constitution of the United States and made up my mind right then and there, to become a citizen. I am a citizen." She put her hand up to halt the beginning of applause. "Let me go back a bit into history. My memories of Yugoslavia, are vivid, and certainly undistorted. I and my parents, my uncles, aunts, cousins and friends, lived and died there."

Jelena sighed, but then was revitalized by the fact that the members of the Board were listening patiently. She looked at her watch. "Good, it is still early and I have a few more things." When she heard David trying to stifle a laugh, she smiled.

"My family lived in communist Yugoslavia, a collection of states whose only common thread was the language spoken there. Before that the Nazi's controlled my country, what is now called Croatia. The monster Tito who ruled Yugoslavia died the year I was born. Therefore, I never knew him, but learned more than I wanted to about him. In school, we were taught what the communists wanted us to learn. This is why I was so interested about what Mr. Ashton, I am sorry. He asked me to call him Stanley. What Stanley said about issues in general about the education system in the U.S., and especially here at the school our children attend. In the school that I attended until I was twelve, if you had doubts or questions, you kept them in your mind, which is if you had a mind that had not been fully brain washed. Here we have the privilege of questioning as we do this evening. If any of us had done that, it would be off to a labor camp along with our parents who could have been innocent. They had our bodies, but thank goodness not our souls."

Jelena had tears in her eyes. "Today, in the country of my birth, Croatia, there have been some changes for the good, but despite economical improvement, it is a country that is run by socialists. The government provides. The government provides much too much." She gathered her thoughts. "

When I came to this country and embraced everything about it, I asked for nothing, but to make my own way." Jelena looked at Sasha. "Still in Croatia, there is a lack of initiative for too many. Hopefully many entrepreneurs will rise up. Some Croatians will absolutely disagree. That is their right."

Jelena took a deep breath. "In conclusion, my message to all of the young people still awake here tonight, is to be what you want to the best of your ability. There are winners. There are losers in this world. Everyone has the chance to rise above the pile, if they are determined to do so. Everyone has the right; I have read the Bill of Rights, and freedom to speak their mind, without censorship, except for certain rare understood circumstances. Young people, do not look to government to be your nanny. You all have parents, hopefully who provide the guidelines to make the choices you will make as you grow. Earn the things you wish to have. They become so more treasured when you do so. Sadly, I see this country moving in a direction that has failed just about all of Europe. You will be able to vote in coming elections. Make the most of that precious right."

She was stunned by the applause, as members of the audience came down to the edge of the stage, not allowing her to leave, while the apoplectic Chairman of the Board saw there was nothing he could do.

Mandy Van Wagoner, Carissa's sister, pushed her ample frame forward. "Speak at our graduation. Please, Mrs., Finkel" and Rabbi Tom called out, "The three of us here just wish to hug you."

Stanley asked Reid Harris if a five-minute break might be in order. He agreed, but only to collect any member of the Board he could depend upon for a brief meeting with Hannah, Gannif, and the teachers.

Once everyone had returned to their seats, Stanley went back to the podium. "We have two more people who have something important to share with you. My daughter Jillian Ashton and Sasha Finkel." Although it had been decided that Jillian would speak first, she insisted that Sasha join her on the stage.

TWENTY-NINE

Jillian

Jillian walked over to the podium, and immediately realized she would not be seen if she stood behind it. She took the microphone from her father and sat down at the edge of the stage, her feet dangling down toward the auditorium floor.

"I guess no one was prepared for shorter people to speak." Some laughter came from the younger members of the audience. "So am going to be informal, even though my message will not be in any way informal, or at all amusing."

"As you all have been told, our Current History teacher, Ms. Davida Jones gave us an assignment to write an essay. We were to consider why, and I quote, 'Barack Obama was to be considered one of the great presidents and leaders of the United States'. As you can see there was little or no wiggle room for anyone to come to a different conclusion. Let me say this. For someone my age, I have been very liberal in my ideas, despite living with a family that is quite conservative. When I was given the assignment, I almost believed I could write what was intended. I was very excited when in November of 2008, a black man was elected president, and believed that real Hope and Change was going to make America a better country for all of its citizens. I discussed the essay with my parents and my brother Mark, and agreed to read every thing I could that was both positive and negative about Mr. Obama and his administration. I have included a syllabus at the end of my essay which, incidentally is available to anyone who wishes to read it."

Jillian tried to find a comfortable spot where she sat, and then got up. "This is hurting my tush, so I will try the podium. Is there a box or short steps back stage?" Malcolm went to find something and returned with a wooden orange crate.

Jillian made certain it would support her weight. "That's better," she said. "Now you can see me above this stand."

She looked at some note cards she had prepared. "So, since I am a member of the school debate club, I decided to treat my essay like a debate, and award points for each issue that I felt important to deal with. President Obama had to give the okay to get bin Laden, even though it was our brave Navy Seals who accomplished it, so for that I awarded that side one point. However as I read more and more, and learned about what happened in Benghazi, the IRS, NSA, and of course with the Affordable Care Act, which even the president refers to as obamacare, the bright lights of Hope and Change dimmed considerably, and points were awarded to the other side. I plan to devote more of this time I have to obamacare. As an aside, it has gone so poorly since the October not so grand opening debacle that Nancy Pelosi does not wish to say the word obamacare. More and more democrats who will seek re-election in 2014 are distancing themselves from it, and the president as well. Points could have been awarded for transparency, since the president assured us that his presidency would be the most transparent. Alas, this is not the case. In order not to provide damaging information that could jeopardize his 2012 re-election, the facts regarding Benghazi were distorted, and promises he made about keeping your healthcare, your doctors and hospitals were lies. No points awarded there. The president, while running for election in 2008, said he planned to reunite America, which so many assumed since he was black, that racism in this country would seemingly dissolve. After all, it took white America to elect him. Should be some points there, but no, it didn't happen. In fact I believe he has done more to energize class warfare with his speeches, but certainly has been right up there when he felt that an Afro-American had been unjustly treated, and fomented anger in the black community. This was not the case when the injured was white."

Jillian looked at her father, who nodded to continue. "The president pledged to improve our economic miseries. Should get a point for that, but he made them worse, by spending taxpayer money on failed so-called green ventures, such as the solar panel manufacturer, Solyndra, and the list goes on and on, if you add the electric cars and windmills."

Stanley brought her a glass of water, and whispered. "You are doing just great." Sasha, off to the side gave her a thumbs up.

"Going back to the Affordable Care Act, it so far has proven to be very expensive. At least 50 million people have lost their health insurance. The young people expected to sign up and bear the brunt of its costs have not. Despite the clever fudging of numbers, the majority of people who signed at least in California, were placed in Medicaid, and provide no financial support to the plan. Those who have been able to access the website, have found their deductibles rise as high as $6000. Democrats claim that Republicans have provided no alternative to obamacare and that is just another lie. Okay, no points there. When a new issue comes up that clearly makes obamacare unworkable, the president has used executive order to provide waivers, exclusions, changes, diversions and delays. No points earned there either."

"I have come to the conclusion that some one who never ran anything, least of all a business, whose only real claim to fame was as a community organizer in Chicago, associating with many people of questionable integrity, was never prepared to be president, or as many put it leader of the free world. He has an agenda to push our health care into a single-payer system, and that is all that obamacare is about. The goal is to turn America into a socialistic state. Our once stellar position in the world has been jeopardized, and contaminated with poor foreign policy decisions and leading from behind."

"Most people honestly believe that President Obama wants to end the wars without winning them. How must the parents of all of the military who lost their lives and limbs in Iraq and Afghanistan feel about this man?"

"Again, looking at the not so affordable healthcare law, and the stated positions of some of the people directly involved in writing it, one gets a sense that people are devalued. The Nazis devalued the Jews of Europe and had their final solution. It seems that obamacare would devalue the lives of some of the very sick and elderly, so that budgets are met and things made to look good."

"In conclusion, I could have written a glowing essay, with an ending acceptable to Davida Jones and the administration, but I could not do that just for the grade. I believe I made my case by debating all of the issues. Isn't that what learning is all about? I deserve a better grade for doing just that, and so do all of my classmates who believing in their right to do so, and wrote essays that were both courageous and truthful."

THIRTY

Sasha

Again, the audience rose to applaud, joined by a number of the members of the Board. Jillian thanked them, and ask that they give Sasha Finkel their complete attention.

Sasha kissed Jillian on the cheek and took the microphone. She pushed away the box with her foot and took place behind the podium. "I think you can see and hear me without that, but right now Jillian Ashton stands taller than any of us." There was again a brief applause that Sasha waited for to die down.

"People know me for expressing myself exactly how I feel. Call it being blunt. I could care less, so do not expect anything different tonight." Sasha said with a smile. "We all had the same opportunity, the classes, that is, to review all of the pros and cons with regard to the accomplishments of president Obama. I will be right up front when I tell you I never trusted him, certainly from what I have read, and listened to at least on television news networks that are unbiased and report the news, as it should be told. I heard him say that he planned to 'fundamentally change this country' and he certainly has, for the worse. I am very conservative in my views and somewhat liberal with regard to having feelings for the so-called have-nots, but I draw the line at government providing free cell phones, and all the stuff the democrats offered in turn for their votes, and God and the democratic party are the only ones who know how many times each of these people voted! Some 40 million people are being given food stamps, and many legitimately require them for survival, but how much of these pieces of paper are exchanged for cash to purchase, drugs, cigarettes, tattoos, piercings, and all of the junk food that the president's wife considers unhealthy. By the way, the cafeteria food sucks."

"When any one questions this or anything the president does, the response from so many democrats is: 'you hate him because he is black. You hate women and children. You would have the needy starve'. That is the only answer they have to give. And when you say anything true, but considered by them, derogatory against the health law, you are told you just don't care if people die. Let us see how true this will be, as the president's appointed fifteen bureaucrats take their seats and make Life and Death decisions based upon age, infirmity and cost effectiveness. Patients would like to have the right to make these medical decisions with their doctors and not the government, which believes Americans are too dumb to do what is right, regarding their health, what they choose to eat, what and when their children should be taught about sex, and what they are taught in school. The latter has already been discussed, and brilliantly, by my mother Jelena Finkel. Now we all know that the health care act when it was a bill before Congress, and not voted for by one Republican, was not read by any one of the people who voted for it. Apparently that is considered the way to go, even by one of the members of the Board seated behind me." Jeanette Pelochi smiled weakly, the best she could, considering.

Speaking of my mother. I have been fortunate to have two mothers. My birth mother, died, when I was barely a toddler, and now Jelena whom I also love dearly, is my mother. I believe in marriage between a man and a woman. How better would members of the minorities fare with children living in a home with both parents? Obamacare provides more assistance to a single unmarried woman, discouraging the presence of the father in the home. Now those who do not believe in traditional marriage will act as their needs and appetites dictate. What I will not accept is their forcing their convictions upon me. This goes as well, for people who are atheists or agnostics. Believing in nothing is nothing at all. The president has done everything to foster their cause, and I would presume for all of the votes it might get, this goes as well for the sudden push for amnesty of illegal immigrants."

"Clearly, another potential bundle of votes. Certainly this has to be dealt with in a reasonable way, but not by a Congress that takes more vacations than it creates and enacts legislation. Jillian spoke about the dearth of foreign policy and the scandals that the administration would like quickly forgotten, but Benghazi will not go way, as assuredly as Hillary Clinton will try to make it disappear."

"So with all of the information provided by everyone who spoke before me, how in the world can anyone give this president a good grade? He is already below 40% approval rate of a job poorly done. We all deserved better from our teacher, but apparently we expected too much." She paused to clear her throat. "This is a good school, that we attend, but it could be a great school. I think we, as students, at least in the upper grades, and our parents, have a right to question the curriculum, as well as the motives of the administration and our educators. We as a free people have the right to be given both sides of any story and not just the one they wish us to hear. We attend school to learn and not to be brainwashed about such stuff as global warming, or fracking. We deserve to be able to come to whatever conclusion we do, as long as we have all of the information with which to do so. We as a people deserve not to be lied to by our president, members of his cabinet, or any of his non-elected appointees. No one should avoid criticizing the president or his policies in fear that they might be labeled a racist. We need more members of the black communities to help their people, rather than keeping them poor and ignorant just for their votes. The president should encourage hard work and achievement, rather than providing an unending supply of entitlements that keeps the people unemployed, lethargic, disinterested and dependent upon government."

"I wanted to include this earlier, but I was so passionate about my concerns, I forgot to do so. It is so important for a child to have a mother and a father with both parents living at home, to stabilize that home. I will underscore this with something that today, came to my attention." Sasha looked down at her hand where she had written something in ink.

"I keep notes in the strangest places." She said with a laugh. Did you know what the percentages are, in this country for children born out of wedlock? I shall tell you. 27% are in the white population, 52% in the Hispanic population and 72% in the Afro-American population. All of this leads to more poverty, speaking of which, since President Johnson created something called the war on poverty, 27 Trillion dollars has been spent to eliminate it since 1964. Certainly looks like money not well spent, since there is significantly more poverty in this country, considering the fact that our population has increased so. When one really considers Johnson's contribution, it was just another entitlement that encouraged promiscuity, and out of wedlock pregnancies because they proved to be money making propositions for those who understood how the tax paying public could be further defrauded. Some years ago, a future United States Senator, after noting that poverty was still in single digits, warned of the dire straits this country would be in if it ever rose significantly. Well, it has, and Senator Moynihan, from our State of New York, was correct."

"I believe the onus is on us to insist that change occur here at Endicott Witherspoon, and it cannot come too soon. We are one year away from graduation and hope, despite what has happened, to get into the colleges and universities of our choice and not by virtue of some governmental back door." She glanced at Davida Jones.

Sasha then turned to look at the members of the Board of Trustees. "I trust that the members of the Board have listened to what all of us have set forth, and make the changes needed to improve this school, and be proud of their accomplishment. But start tomorrow. Not next month. 2014 is almost here. Make your first important resolution now, and please keep it."

The audience began to applaud and cheer, but Sasha yelled over it. "You think I regret anything I have said? Hell no!

Stanley, a broad grin framing his face, asked if any one else wished to speak. He turned to the Board members and asked them the same question. Malcolm rose from his seat.

"It will take some time to completely digest everything that has been said or the challenges provided. I personally wish to thank Jelena, Sasha, Jillian, and certainly Stanley and David Finkel for making tonight happen. It obviously was very important that this town meeting occurred. As Sasha said, we are coming to the end of the semester and this year as well. I for one will insist that the specific essay assigned, as well as the manner in which it was graded be revisited with the administration, the teacher in question, along with the Board, to see if any adjustments should be forthcoming. I want to thank all of you who came and stayed so late to hear what had to be said."

Malcolm turned toward Reid Harris who just stared angrily at Dean Hannah and Davida Jones. "Reid, why don't you bang that hand gavel and end this meeting. Despite the fact that the hour is late and many of us are tired, we have to meet tonight for as long as it takes to nominate Board members for next year. This was never done and this year, as I said is coming to an end. Both Thornton and I have decided to call this emergency meeting since we are all in attendance." He looked at Dean Hannah. "You, Sir and your faculty members are excused. Murray, would you like to sit with rest of us now?"

Stanley asked for a moment before the audience left the hall. "I have kept this for last, hoping I would have good news to give you all, and I have." The people appeared bewildered. "Late this afternoon, Victoria Morales, for a reason, her parents believe had to do with the failing grade she received, took pills she found in their room. Fortunately they found her in time and called the squad. Father Anthony just handed me a note that Victoria will be fine, and that her mother wanted me to tell you what happened."

THIRTY-ONE

Resolution

Reid Harris was furious. "How dare you do such a thing, Dick? After all support the school and I personally have given you for your political career? I am chairman of this Board and will call Board meetings when I deem necessary. This entire circus you engineered tonight was absurd with these young brats, and that woman, pontificating about matters of which she knows little! We are adjourned!" He started to rise from his seat when Thornton Dick placed a firm hand on his shoulder.

"Malcolm, perhaps you should advise the Chairman about decisions made. And while you are at it, show him the page in the By-laws, that I guess he has not read either, that if a majority of the Board deems it necessary to call an emergency meeting, he or she can do so." Thornton Dick said.

Malcolm Storey brought his copy and placed it in front of Reid Harris, pointing to a paragraph he had underlined. "You see Mr. Chairman, you created a nominating committee to determine which members of the Board are to be held over depending upon their established terms. I might remind you Mr. Chairman, that your term in that capacity ends this year, unless you are re-elected." Malcolm said.

"Well," Reid Harris said indignantly, "since I am still Chairman, I shall continue to run this committee, and am not calling for the matter to be discussed."

"I then," said Thornton Dick, "make a motion to bring up the needs of this Board to do diligence, and consider the recommendations of the nominating committee for the coming year as to the composition of this Board of Trustees."

"As Chairman, I can decide to do nothing of the kind." Harris said with a smirk.

"Actually, that is not the case as Murray Gannif will tell you, if asked. In order not to have a dictatorial position taken by the Chairman, as we all have see occur in our United States Senate, you must also have failed to note the portion of the By-Laws that stipulate that, if a majority of the Board desires it to be voted on, so be it." Malcolm offered.

Reid Harris looked at Murray Gannif who indicated that was correct.

"There are actually eighteen members of this Board who agree with us, and since the New Year is looming, the matter of the nominating committees determination must be dealt with, tonight." Thornton Dick advised.

"You really have eighteen members, many of whom are my friends who will go against my wishes?" Harris asked.

"As they say, it isn't personal." Malcolm said.

"I stand with you, Reid," Murray Gannif said, "and I know Jeanette will also."

Reid Harris looked at Jeanette Poliche, who looked down at her hands. "Actually, I hope to remain on the Board." She looked at Malcolm. "It was their doing, Harris and Gannif, to do anything to get that damn government grant for the school. Lots of things pass by me as Secretary and Treasurer of the Board, and an audit might be in order" She said, beginning to cry.

"Shut up Jeanette!" Gannif yelled. You will get us all in trouble, and you as well since you are just as culpable." Gannif suddenly realized he also should have remained silent."

"They needed the money to make up for shortfalls," Poliche said through sobs.

"That explains a lot of things." Malcolm said. "We have a motion, and if there is no more discussion, I ask for vote by the raising of hands." The vote was eighteen to two in favor of bringing the nominations up for a vote, with two nays and one abstention."

"Now, Mr. Chairman, it is up to you." Thornton Dick said as he handed out a paper to each member of the Board.

Defeated, Reid Harris tossed the paper containing the selections of the Nominating Committee, which consisted of Thornton, Malcolm and Bill Klein, away.

The Board voted to elect Bill Klein Chairman for a two-year period, Thornton Dick, Secretary and Malcolm Storey, Treasurer for the same time period. Murray Gannif, Reid Harris and Jeanette Poliche were not asked to return, and were advised that the school's books would be audited by an independent firm, and anyone ultimately found to be in any way involved in anything illegal would be appropriately dealt with. It was also determined that Stanley Ashton would be asked if he would be willing to serve on the Board.

"We need an influx of new Board members who will come with good ideas to make this school what it should be, and not just those who come only to eat lunch while contributing nothing. Our next effort at the first meeting in January of 2014, will be to look carefully at the Dean, his administration and any members of the teaching faculty as to what necessary changes must be made." Bill Klein took the gavel and emphatically banged the meeting to a close.

EPILOGUE

The audit revealed that a considerable amount of money could not be accounted for. As the former Board member and Secretary and Treasurer, Jeanette Poliche, who admitted to signing checks, for payments of which she had no knowledge, was found to be guilty of incompetence and stupidity. She was placed on probation for three years and had to perform community service.

It was concluded that Dean Hannah had no direct part in the fraudulent activities. He resigned. Had he not done so, he would have be provided with a "transitional job" or have his ass fired as stated by Bill Klein who was not politically correct. When last heard of, he was working in a Big Box store in Maryland.

Davida Jones stayed on under a probationary period for three months, until a new teacher had been hired. She had no tenure. A detailed evaluation of the performances of both Edgar Fluecke and Vernon Jarretts contributed to their termination at the school.

Murray Gannif and Reid Harris were indicted for conspiracy to defraud and misuse of school funds. Harris pled guilty and was ordered to pay back an amount of money with interest. The judge sentenced him to jail for five years, but because of his age, placed him in a low level penal institution, not far from where he lived, to make it easier for his ailing wife to visit. Gannif skipped bail, since he for some reason, had not been considered a flight risk. He is believed to have fled to one of the smaller of the Bahama Islands, living under an assumed name at a villa allegedly owned by a New York Congressman.

Stanley and Jennie Ashton became disenchanted with living in New York, after the Governor suggested that there was no place in New York State for any one who disagreed with him on gun control, abortion and marriage, and after a great deal of soul searching relocated to Shelby, North Carolina, a small town near the border of South Carolina in the western part of the state. There they would be close enough to Charlotte, where they could enjoy its southern culture, restaurants and entertainment. Jennie found a job at an Assisted Living Home in Shelby, while Stanley joined a small law firm where he could work a few days a week without having to litigate in court.

After the Board of Trustees and the new Administration reviewed the essays and gave more appropriate grades for effort and content, those members of the junior class were able to make application to the colleges and universities of their choice. Jillian received acceptance to a number of schools but George Mason was her first choice, and had made it her school for early decision. She wanted to major in political science and felt the Washington area was the perfect place to live and learn. After graduation, she went on to Georgetown School of Law and graduated with honors. She worked for the Republican Committee to re-elect the president in 2020, and the country in an effort to maintain the good economy, and all the gains made in domestic and foreign relations, re-elected the former Arkansas Governor to his second term.

Malcolm Storey's practice continued to grow, as obamacare, as expected, went belly up. America breathed a sigh of relief, when in the 2014 midterm elections, the Republican party won the House and the Senate, with enough votes to override a presidential veto. The Affordable Care Act was repealed and replaced with a sensible alternative. With fewer lawyers in the legislature, tort reform became a reality, people could cross state lines to purchase health insurance, and all decisions regarding diagnosis and treatment were again to be decided by the patient and his doctor.

The only part of obamacare that was kept and restructured was the issue of pre-existing conditions. However it would be understood that those premiums would be slightly higher.

Kelly Storey, having decided to become a social worker, graduated from the NYU School of Social Work. She currently is the assistant to the head of Social Services at Kingston Hospital, is married, and has kept in contact with Sasha and Jillian.

David Finkel chose to stay and practice in Kingston, New York, and he agreed to become a member of the school's Board of Trustees. Jelena's dance school attracted many students, a few who were accepted to be in the chorus of the New York Ballet. Upon her insistence, David relented and purchased a summer home in Deal at the Jersey shore, where they would be able to spend time with Sasha.

Sasha Finkle graduated summa cum laude from Bard College, just across the Hudson River. She was accepted at Albert Einstein in the Bronx, but elected to go to the Rutgers School of Medicine in New Brunswick, New Jersey where she graduated first in her class. Sasha decided upon a fellowship in Pediatric rehabilitation, which was newly offered at the Robert Wood Johnson Rehabilitation Hospital, a part of the JFK Medical Center, located in nearby Edison. She was also aware of the fact that Dr. Mark Ashton had accepted a job in the Department of Radiology there. After all, her Dad was ten years older than Jelena, and that seem to work out just fine.

Authors Note

This novel, while a work of fiction, contains information culled from daily events, which I felt appropriate to use since without them, this book could not have been written. None of the characters are real. They all are inventions of my imagination. While the hamlets of Hurley and Woodstock are located in upstate, New York, the Agnes Endicott Witherspoon Preparatory School does not and never did exist, so therefore the teachers, administration and Board of Trustees, never existed as well. But, they could have. The opinions of the characters in his book are theirs and theirs alone. Any similarity between them and the living or dead is purely coincidental.

As a physician and pediatrician, I have great concerns for the direction our delivery of quality health has taken. It is not going well. The government should never have interfered in what has always been sacrosanct: the relationship between a doctor and his patient. It is blatantly apparent that the current president, his administration, his advisors, and many members of his party, envision a single-payer system for the people of the United States. Which, as Jillian Ashton noted has not worked well in Europe or Canada. This readily apparent by reviewing the comparative statistics concerning cancer rates and cures, along with the timeliness with which a patients can see his or her physician when urgent care or surgeries are required. Certainly, this country far excels in these areas and many more. Why would any one wish to tamper with them unless there were ulterior motives?

With regard to education, despite how much money has been provided, America's children rank far behind so many countries, and the illogical answer continues to be to provide more and more funding, without attempting to improve the quality of the educators, without rewarding good efforts from the best, and giving tenure to some of the worst.

The characters in this novel have spelled out clearly their feelings about what they do and do not expect from government. A good start would be with honesty.

Quotable Quotes

"Instead of giving a politician the keys to the city, it might be better to change the locks."

Attributed to Doug Larson

"When I was a boy I was told that anybody could become President; I'm beginning to believe it."

Attributed to Clarence Darrow

Woodstock, New York

Review with your children and their teachers, the concept of THE COMMON CORE, a standardization of education now being taught in public schools. While exhibiting some merit, there is no place in K-12 for political indoctrination, brainwashing or promotion of propaganda.

*IF YOU HAVE PURCHASED THIS BOOK, FEEL FREE TO WRITE YOUR OWN ESSAY ON ANY OF THE TOPICS COVERED, ON THE FOLLOWING PAGES.

AN ACKNOWLEDGEMENT

I would be remiss in not acknowledging the great contribution Fox Cable News, and all of its anchors make in providing clear and unbiased news. It is no wonder that certain people are hostile to Fox because of its continued effort to determine with whom the responsibility for the murders in Benghazi lie, and to maintain pressure to find the truth regarding the scandals involving the IRS the NSA, and Fast and Furious, just to mention a few of many.

ESSAY: PAGE ONE

ESSAY: PAGE TWO

ESSAY: PAGE THREE

ESSAY: PAGE FOUR

ESSAY: PAGE FIVE

ESSAY: PAGE SIX

ESSAY: PAGE SEVEN

ESSAY: PAGE EIGHT